to Pascoe

with th
passion
hopes that
this in

Ellen

Auto

by Ellen Rugen

For my children Naomi and Rowan
and my grandchildren
Imogen and Earon

ISBN-13: 978-1494958862
ISBN-10: 1494958864

There are several reasons for writing a life. I think of writing to remember – to remember for a future when I may not be able to remember much. My grandchildren may want to know something of what went before. Their lives have overlapped with mine but there is nothing of them in this memoir. Likewise there is little of my daughter even though she is very important to me. But this is a reflection on my own chronology. I have a mind to write something more meaningful, yet I also have a sense of time running out. Recently a couple of acquaintances have said in response to some experience I have mentioned, 'You have had an interesting life.' And so this chronicle may be read a little outside the family.

One problem in writing about what may have happened is that one inevitably refers to other people. People may not wish to be mentioned, or conversely they may feel hurt that they have been left out. Did they mean so little?

There is some satisfaction in making what seemed haphazard at the time become a coherent story. There is finally the sheer pleasure of writing and creating a book only made possible by the technological revolution.

Villembits 2014

1

Growing Up

I came with the flying bombs

As long as the bombs droned they were going somewhere…. else. Silence….. They dropped straight down. They often landed on and around Hampstead where my parents were renting a flat, so my mother escaped to her parents in Manchester, a few months before I was dragged into the world by forceps. My father, an income tax inspector stayed in London and played his part in the Home Guard. The landlady did not want to have her nights further disturbed by a crying baby and my parents left London soon after my birth, just as the war was ending. Possibly with idealistic notions of the good life, they made for rural Buckinghamshire.

Age 2-4

We lived in a chocolate- box -thatched cottage: it was condemned. The rent was 17 shillings a week. We had a tiger left by the previous tenants – a reserved creature who perched and ate and disappeared out. There was a phone line to the landlord, and a large rambling garden where my father grew strawberries and artichokes. The cottage was at the end of a row and beyond lay woods. Alongside were The Neighbours. Abutting the house (forming an L shape to the row was a post office). There was plenty of space for parking the Ford 8.

As I approached 4 years old I played out with Jill who lived next door. Her family kept chickens. We were free to explore – the woods, our bodies, and the small world we inhabited.

In the early morning on my birthday my mother left out a present which I crept down to see. It was her precious porcelain doll. I don't remember having any special thoughts about dolls. More importantly it was hers and in giving it to me I felt a responsibility to look after her. She had a delicate complexion and eyes that opened and closed. Somehow – I don't know how- she lay on the floor with a broken head. My mother was devastated and although the doll's hospital put her back together, I never did like dolls before or since.

My mother regarded herself a cut above the neighbours. Indeed she came from a cultured Jewish family in Manchester about as far as you could get from rural Buckinghamshire. She was isolated and depressed. My father left early to commute to work in the City and reappeared after I had gone to bed. I would lie awake waiting for him to arrive for my story. He made them up. I remember a character called Scatterwitch though nothing sticks of his adventures. I remember the occasional trip into High Wycombe wearing my strokable furry mittens. My mother stocked up on brown packets about six by four inches and 3 inches deep. 'Towels' she said. But I never quite believed her – 'You don't get towels that small do you?' She once branched out into a perm. This was one of her worst days. She was largely unrecognisable and stood in front of the mirror as if by continuously pulling and combing it would go away. She hated housework and she hated being followed around. In despair one day she shut me in the cottage whilst she got a few minutes to herself putting the washing on the line. I was desperate and managed to climb on the table, open the window and prepare to jump out. She saw me just in time.

Before Jill became part of my life I was very much a solitary child. I learnt to amuse myself. The large armchair was rectangular and could easily be converted to a number of shelters or forms of transport. I had a basket of toys – my treasures - next to the fireplace. On the other side was the bread oven.

I slept in my cot until a late age. In the last year at Radnage I graduated to a bed – a grown up single bed. This transition was delayed because I regularly wet the bed at night. I enjoyed the feeling of being swaddled in wet warmth. But the washing must have been too much for my mother. She did not enjoy cooking either. Her childhood experience had been of a ritualised diet – roast on Saturday, cold on Sunday, fish on Friday and I don't know what inbetween. When she got married the only thing she knew how to cook was a poached egg.

By the time I met her mother – Granny- she was, in her sixties, virtually an invalid sitting unloved in her armchair. I played at being cute and she was amused and gave me half a crown on the few occasions we went to visit. My grandmother had stayed in bed for a month after giving birth which she managed only twice. My mother and her sister had wet nurses followed by nannies. Granny's mother had died when she was five, and her sister seven, in Poland in the 1880's. There was no great tradition of mothering in the family.

Manchester was a day away. My first memory is my second birthday in my grandparent's house. I was lying in my cot looking up at my aunt, mother and other relatives. Another time my mother took me there on the train – a steam train– with seats which flipped up hiding my mother's lipstick which I had dropped down there.

My early childhood was dominated by the question of MILK it seemed. My mother had strong views that I must drink a good mugful at breakfast. But the milk that was available in rural post-war Bucks, was unpasteurised and therefore had to be boiled. It was something I detested. I sat there for what seemed like hours not drinking, and she was equally obstinate that it had to be drunk. Another trial of the day was the WALK. This constitutional was at first taken in a large pushchair but all too soon I was expected to walk on my own two legs. And I grumbled at the boring passage of grass and hedgerows going nowhere except where we had started.

Light relief came in the form of visitors. Granny and Grandpa came once or twice. Then there was my aunt who liked to ride horses and arranged for me to sit on one whilst it walked around. Having no children of her own did not deter her, as my mother's elder sister, from having plenty of ideas about how to manage her niece and my mother found this irksome in the extreme. The greatest event, from my mother's point of view, was a visit from her best friend who had settled in Buenos Aires and was over for a visit. They wrote long letters to each other frequently on crackling airmail paper. Esmée had a son Philip a few years older than me and annoyingly able, and allowed, to do things I could not.

One day I was to be left with the neighbour at the far end of the row. We approached the house but my sense of panic grew by the second. Looking into the door all I could see was a black hole. I became frantic and yet again my mother got no respite. There was nothing for it but to take me back with her.

Another time a strange boy was left with us to play - with me I thought. It turned out, however, that MY MOTHER played with him. There was a miniature, perhaps travelling, box of draughts– something quite beyond me. As they played I became more and more furious until finally I struck out and the game went flying.

The Christmas tree went up to the ceiling. My father cut a branch from the row of evergreens outside. There was a glossy dark brown and gold chocolate bar on it and a fairy on the top. There were paper decorations in the room and it was altogether a wonderful time. The stocking which I found in my cot had a tangerine in the toe. My father was particularly fond of one of the toys which Father Christmas had brought – a hollow stick through which you could blow up a balloon. In his excitement he blew too hard and the balloon burst. I didn't really mind.

I was oblivious to the vicissitudes of life as I became ill with whooping cough after my father caught pneumonia in the exceptionally cold winter in '47. I did not share my mother's horror as the septic tank regurgitated its contents in the bathroom. I was entertained rather than distraught when a hole appeared in the wall. I was in my cot one evening when I was aware of a small hole growing in the wall next to me. It enabled me to peer down into the neighbour's sitting room next door.

The day came to say goodbye to Jill. The removal van came to put our things in store. We were going to my mother's most favourite place – the Lakes. My father had engineered a transfer and in the short term this was to be my mother's best year – no housework, a husband working within walking distance, a child beginning school and for much of the time played with and adored by the other hotel residents. Additionally she could attend midday concerts, and do a spot of music teaching in her friend's little Frobelian school. For a short time I exchanged postcards with Jill.

Age 4-5

My father's transfer to Kendal combined with my first days at school lasted a relatively short time but seems very important. We lived for most of one year in a small family hotel where I was the only child. There were several elderly ladies– Mrs Price, and Mrs Cannon I remember especially (Mrs or Miss? They were in their 80's – birth around 1870.) I lapped up their attention and duly received gifts – a silk parasol, painted feather fans. Consequently the average age of the people who came to my 5th birthday party was about 70. The hotel had a number of people who passed through as well as some other semi-permanent guests. It had many of the aspects of living in a community and perhaps was the source of my interest in that way of living. To complete the idyll, my first school was in the ground floor of the Victorian mansion next door and the teacher was one of my mother's best friends, Flo. Flo was a single woman with no children of her own and yet an immense capacity to enter into a child's world born not only from a lifetime of her professional work with children but of an intuitive ability which allowed her to treat children as persons in their own right.

My mother was in her element. She could play Bach preludes in the lounge and her wit and intelligence were valued. My father walked to work and came home soon after Childrens' Hour which I listened to in solitude whilst eating my tea– invariably a plain egg salad. Only towards the end of the year was I allowed to attend the hotel evening meal where we sat on a table with Guy – a young accountant who for some unaccountable and unintentional reason caused me to giggle uncontrollably. Guy and the family kept in touch and when my parents died years later, I exchanged wry letters with him at Christmas. It was not until some half a century later that I made the trip to see him where he then lived in Ireland having been adopted by a loving family as a surrogate grandparent. Through that year we maintained monthly phone calls until one month I could not get hold of him. I was glad I had made that last trip.

My mother was able to claim her rightful role as a musician. The highlight of the week for her was the midday concert in a hall in Kendal where she sometimes rose to the dizzy rank of page turner for the performer. I sat through many of these concerts and have loathed most classical music ever since. She was horrified one time to find me trying out my new skill of whistling to pass the time away.

After some time we moved into rented accommodation – the house next door to the hotel the other way. This was the house of Connie Geldard– an active elderly lady who wore pointed shoes and purple. We had furnished rooms in her house whilst our furniture was in store. (This conjured up a picture of a grain store with a lot of hay.) Our sitting room was at the front on the ground floor, my parent's bedroom was next to her sitting room on the first floor and my bedroom was next to hers on the top floor. Above this was a staircase which opened up a further world – the attic. Our sitting room had a goldfish bowl with brightly coloured glass fish. There was a long terraced garden where I developed a taste for making posies and one day I committed the ultimate sin of picking a white flower with a yellow centre. I wept long and hard when I learnt that this flower would have become a strawberry.

At school we were given papier maché blue eggs on a yellow base. I put half my sixpence pocket money in every week. Every now and again I earned a bluebird badge. This was for the League of Pity- a charity for poor children. I was more concerned with the acquisition of the trappings than with the cause itself. I befriended a rather sad little boy who had terrible eczema all over his legs which were exposed below his short trousers. But after a term or two he went away. I also had a friend Rose who was as beautiful as her name. She lived some distance away and I visited her farm only once. It was near Sellafied and like a cluster of children in that area, tragically, she was to die as a teenager of leukaemia and nuclear power.

Connie Geldard's house was the first of some half a dozen terraced houses and there were several more grand old ladies to entertain and be entertained by. My mother made friends with them all and we were in and out of each others houses a great deal. I liked Mrs Wilson's garden best as it stretched on a gentle slope downwards with only grass and trees

I was bright and soon picked up the shapes and sounds of words, and happily worked at my own pace through the sum books. Socially I was, however, a little backward and also given to experimentation. As we sat in a circle and in turn made our contribution I wondered idly what would happen if I withdrew the chair of the girl next to me when she stood up to speak. She of course sat down into space and I got a shocked pained look. Still Hilary became a friend and was allowed on several occasions to come to tea though I doubt I knew what to do with her. It was more fun at her house because she had brothers and sisters, more toys and a dedicated playroom.

I also made an important discovery and flew back home one lunchtime to tell my mother that there existed in the sky a person who was all the time looking after us. How could she not have known this important fact? She was not as excited as I was. Still there began my relationship with Connie Geldard's church. We – Connie and I– set off together every Sunday morning without fail and I was entranced by her crackling prayer book and the singing of the choir boys especially when there was a solo.

It was the time of the Festival of Britain and our little school competed in a choir competition and another musical event. There was our picture in the paper. It was my mother who taught music and also French. This was a mixed blessing. I was outraged when she brought in one of MY books to read to the class and had to be put in Flo's class whilst I calmed down.

Soon I was allowed to stay at school in the afternoon as well. We made bread. We made bird tables. We made clay pots. It took me many attempts to paint within lines and I was somewhat put off painting because of lack of success. This school of some twenty pupils were a close-knit group. We had adventures where we went in search of the source of a stream. Flo then made books of the expedition for us to colour in. My report for this year says 'She does not easily tolerate those who are less able than herself.'

My father, who perhaps would have preferred a son, encouraged outdoor pursuits. I was to be proud, he said, of having reached the top of Hellvelyn at the age of 5. I remember it was a trial lightened only by my father's storytelling and Scatterwitch's ability to have a cliffhanger as the way got steeper. I also remember climbing up the side of the limestone quarry near the hotel on the golf course and balancing on precarious footholds.

One day I arrived back from school to find my mother in an especially foul mood. We were to move again. My father had been transferred to Rochdale – a place that evidently filled my mother with horror combined with grief at leaving. Unable to empathise with her fears and depression I just had a sense that something different was around the corner.

Rochdale Age 6-10

My parents now aged 39 and 40 bought their first house in Norden a little outside Rochdale. It was a 30's semi with square bay windows, two bedrooms and a spare. We had a party phone line with next door and I had my own bedroom. My mother wrote in her diary that the cost of the house (£2,500) suggested that 'the bricks were smeared with platinum'! (She often felt 'poor' and envied her friend in South America who could afford new curtains in her newly built residence.)

I made two friends- the next door dog and Negley- who lived on the other side of our lane which was 'Not Maintained'. This meant it was a bit of a track. Where our lane left the road was another lane – Clay Lane – and much was the scope for exploring and wandering.

Shandy the dog next door- was a rare breed with a very long coat. I played with him in his garden which I reached by climbing over the fence. I really treated him like a person with whom I could romp around and play hide and seek. I invented all sorts of games I could play by myself with a ball against the wall. I also developed a liking for the radio, particularly the afternoon play but also a serial story called 'Journey into Space'.

In an attempt to replicate the Kendal school, I was put in a small private school in Rochdale. It was there that I read my first 'long book'- 'The Secret Mountain' by Enid Blyton. From then on I became an avid reader. Every Saturday I accompanied my father to the local library and chose books which I buried myself in over the weekend. After about the age of 8, I was allowed to take a bus into Rochdale and wander round the town – I especially liked the indoor et. (Either I misremember this or the world was a much safer place.)Towards the end of those years I took out biographies such as Albert Schweizer as well as fiction. I read some classics - such as the Moonstone by Wilkie Collins but also a lot of stories. I then took to writing stories myself. This was much encouraged by my father who gave me threepence for every page I wrote.

I spent only two terms in the private school. It was not a place that was at all exciting and my parents didn't consider that spending most afternoons stencilling was a good use of my time. There were two classes much as in the Kendal school and I was in the older one. The school dinners were a trial and I remember chewing for the best part of an afternoon a sausage skin which I didn't feel I could spit out. It was, however, my first experience of television as we all sat down in front of Mrs Provis' set to watch the funeral of King George the 6th

I was sent some 5 miles away to the junior department of a huge school– Bury Grammar. Here, now aged 6, I was in a terrifying, grim, place. Everything was on a vast scale: - from the pegs where we put our outdoor clothes to the hall which divided after morning assembly to form two rooms- the kindergarten and my class (Transition B); to the large number of children in my class and to the outside space which we shared with the 'big' girls after lunching opposite the road in a huge dining room where we queued up for our school dinners. This class had not learned to do joined up writing yet and I carefully undid my writing to be on a par. I suffered at the beginning where I was on a table with children who were just starting to read. However, after a short time I was transferred to the top table. After assembly, the day began with a chant of all the times-tables. We had one or two lessons with other teachers. I enjoyed the music, and the music room where we went to sing was more informal and intimate than the classroom. I think older girls came to look after us in playtime on the dismal expanse of asphalt which doubled as a several netball courts.

At first my mother came every day to collect me from school. But it was not long before I joined with a couple of other girls who lived, if not near me, in the same direction. The mothers rotated their watch until they felt we could manage the first leg of the journey on a school bus to within a few of miles of home ourselves. By 8, however, I was managing both legs to and from school. This involved changing buses from a local bus to the school bus. Eventually this became a jolly occasion and we little girls used to ride on the top and tease and torment the older boys or indulge in the latest craze: one such was twisting different coloured plastic threads to make a skein.

One day, however – Founders day – for which we had rehearsed long and hard– my first bus missed the school bus and I stood at the bus stop in the middle of nowhere not knowing what to do. A kindly man saw my distress and invited me into his car where there was a convenient bag of sweets. I explained my predicament- I just ***had*** to get to school – and he took me there himself – fortunately! Another mishap occurred when my father drove me a little too late to the bus stop and then raced to catch the departing school bus. He overtook it and in my haste I opened the car door prematurely and fell out in front of the bus. Unscathed I simply got on but there was a call later on that morning– my mother had come to see if I was all right. By that time I was in the next class – Miss Almond's – and had worked out how to be teacher's pet. I was expected to do well and so I did. It was before there was any peer backlash about doing well. There was a paper ladder on the wall and different assignments caused our little personal flag to move up.

The next class was the last before the boys disappeared to the school next door. I was sorry to lose my competition with Peter Greenhalgh as to who was top of the class. By now we sat in our own desks in rows and Peter and I swapped our positions from time to time – the last two desks on the right hand back row. Perhaps in anticipation of this loss, I spent a lot of time playing with the boys – one favourite was making mud - slides down the banking. But the gap they left behind was more than compensated for when a whole batch of new girls arrived including a friend I had made at the earlier private school. She lived in a farm on the moor and occasionally I went to her house for a day in the holidays when she let me ride her horse – Shamrock.

Age 8 was my first experience of separation from my parents. A lady on leave from teaching in Baghdad offered to take away three children of her acquaintance together with a young woman of 20. My parents must have leapt at the chance. I have no idea what my mother did but my father took off for Iceland. Our party – two slightly older boys, myself, Rita and the lady from Baghdad made the long journey to Cornwall by train and I remember the sensation as we passed through Devon of riding on the sea. We arrived at a hut on a cliff after catching a boat near Plymouth. Although I liked Rita, I felt completely lost and much of the week was spent distracting me from homesickness. The daughter of the landlord came to play with me from Plymouth and instead of sleeping in the army style camp bed which I found utterly alarming and not a bed at all I was allowed to sleep in the double bed with Rita. The hut had no electricity and water had to be fetched from lower down the cliff. These huts now I have recently discovered are all modernised and go at a premium rate being situated in an idyllic spot with a mile of beach below.

At school I was keen on rounders. A group of us played every lunch time. Less innocently a gang of us worked out ways to stay inside hiding behind coats in the cloakroom or on a more exploratory note hiding in the toilets and spying on the big girls over the top of the cubicle. Girl power was quite heady and fun and complemented the many books about girls in boarding schools having a whale of a time in the 'dorms', midnight feasts etc.

School became my place of choice and long were the school holidays.

My mother (father went along with this) had a passion for the Lake District from which she now suffered withdrawal symptoms. Hence summer holidays always included a spell there. The most ambitious holiday involved renting a mansion with its own bit of beach on Lake Windermere and having friends to share each of the four separate weeks. The enterprise involved employing an au pair – a teacher training student. It was great to have an older sister for a while and plenty of space to roam. My mother, however, found it not easy to host the many visitors and supervise catering and housekeeping though I am sure everyone mucked in to some extent. There was a tennis court there and I was keen to learn. There was also a squash court. (Some fifty years later, I was surprised to see a picture of the house in 'The Week' where it was advertised as a hotel for a weekend break).With my clipped fringe and short hair I looked and felt very 'plain'- an adjective I heard my mother using to describe me. The daughter of one of my mother's friends – Carla – on the other hand was a natural blond with long glamorous legs. With my fair skin and before the advent of sun cream, I suffered from the sun and went to bed with smarting skin only partly relieved by calamine lotion. Despite bodily concerns, it was a memorable summer.

Norden was a relatively short distance from Prestwich and a Saturday visit to my grandparents became built into the Rochdale routine. When my grandparents moved to Prestwich in 1929, it was a salubrious suburb in North Manchester. By the time I knew it, it had become a gloomy sort of place ridden with traffic and a row of rundown shops. Saturday morning was Granpa's time to go to synagogue. He came home to a good roast dinner which we must have shared many times. I giggled through the Hebrew prayers which seemed to be gabbled gobblygook. After eating too much we whiled away the afternoon until tea time when Aunty Etty (my grandmother's sister) joined us. On winter evenings we went home in the dark.

My grandfather was a small humble man with that essential Jewish ability to look on the world's foibles with a kindly amused eye. He could tell stories and jokes well and he had a marvellous ability to relate to children. He was adored by his daughters – my mother and aunt Connie and in turn by myself and my brother but did not, in my time, have any ability to lighten up my grandmother with whom he shared a bed to the end . He was the first child to be born in this country in a family of thirteen. In 1876, the family had moved from Lisbona house in Damascus. Rumour had it that Edward the 6th had spent the night there. (Recently I saw on the Internet the interior of a book about hidden treasures of Damascus and Lisbona House did indeed look magnificent.) My great grandfather, Moses, had decided to migrate to what was the centre of the world's textile industry. The Sephardi Jews considered themselves superior to the Russian and Polish Jews – the Ashkenazis- who had had a restricted life owing to the pogroms they suffered in Eastern Europe. So his marriage to my maternal grandmother of Polish origin was not approved. She in turn disapproved of my mother's marriage 'out of the faith' (even though it was to an Oxford graduate) and refused to attend their registry office wedding. I like to think that these disapproved- of- marriages gave me a wish to continue to create bridges.

The biggest event of the Rochdale era, however, was my mother caving in to demands from my father and myself to have another child. The first attempt failed and she went into hospital with a miscarriage. The following year (I was nine) she produced my brother. My first impression of him was that he was rather big for a baby. Many were the evenings I spent in the hall pushing his large sprung pram to and fro to get him off to sleep. Another addition to the family was a ginger kitten 'Chips'. My Great Aunt Victoria at that time lived in North Manchester. She was someone I was to get to know in my teenage years when we both lived in Didsbury. All I knew then was that she kept ginger cats and Chips came from her brood. Sadly Chips was with us only two years before he was knocked down by a car and although my mother took him immediately at night to the vet, it was felt kinder to put him down than mend his broken jaw.

At Christmas in my eighth year, surrounded by my relations and all the paraphernalia of a secular Christmas I pontificated on the sins of the Jews who had crucified Christ. The wind was quite taken out of my sails when said relations looked at me sadly and pointed out that they were Jews and that indeed so was I.

About this time I demanded to know where babies came from. I noted that my parents found this profoundly embarrassing and my mother took me upstairs to my room to give me a rudimentary guide to the facts of life.

In the last year of junior school, life became more serious. It began with a dragon of a teacher who maintained an iron hand and fiercely refused to give out any approval for anything to anybody. Composition consisted of sitting down to write to a title for a protracted period of time. The ing was draconian – one never got more than 4+ out of ten – and a tick was given for any slightly out of the ordinary word. My compositions thus make very odd dictionary-led reading. Mercifully for us, though not for her, death felled her midway and we then had a motley array of supply teachers. Craft and painting had vanished on the curriculum. Our class room was alongside the senior school in a separate corridor from the juniors. We were also being prepared for various examinations- entrance to the seniors, and the state 11+ both of which demanded a whole different approach via intelligence tests. We leafed through swathes of symbols to try to imagine what was expected in an answer and a language and a way of thinking that was totally alien. On the basis of these tests we were judged intelligent or not! In my case I had an additional test for a school in South Manchester .When I was not offered a place my mother argued that I had been entered for places reserved for children who were 'out of area' whereas I was about to be very much in area. She won her case.

Yes it was time to move on. My father was promoted to the Manchester office and although he could have commuted from Rochdale, my mother couldn't wait to move – this time to a larger semi in Didsbury. I dragged my feet, very reluctant to lose the opportunity of moving up to the Grammar school. I had to leave my coterie of school friends together with the possibility of being an 'old', rather than, 'new', girl.

Didsbury Age 11-16

This period of my life seemed and seems very long. The new school had all the hiccups that could be expected. The friends I made in my first year were extremely important. I had a school friend Rosemary in my class, and a home friend, Anne, who was in the parallel class. There were new subjects and crisp new exercise books. There was the school assembly with an alarming headmistress and prefects. Education was exclusively didactic and perhaps for that reason so forgettable. In the music lesson we sat in alternate chairs and repeated soullessly the lines of the song played by the teacher. I warmed to the practical-bunsen burners and mysterious liquids changing colour for mysterious scientific reasons. We had a good grounding in sewing and cookery. I did well in so far as I could remember things in a rote learning sort of way. I even turned out the odd good piece of prose informed perhaps by my serious reading habit.

Life settled into a routine not only on school days but also at weekends as I was a very organised sort of person. I walked to school with Anne and saved the bus fare. One evening a week I went to Guides, which most weekends involved an outdoor activity of some sort: lighting fires being an especial favourite. Saturday mornings I went to the Manchester museum with Rosemary to draw. It was not so much a class as a resource centre. There were portable canvas seats and paper and we could go anywhere in the museum we liked. Various teachers came round from time to time to see what we were up to. We drew Egyptian mummies, all sorts of animals and snakes in the aquarium. I did this for a couple of years and was most flattered when aged 12 a teacher asked when I was going to do my GCE art. In the afternoons I went to tea with Aunty Victoria (Great aunt Victoria of the ginger cats). She was my grandfather's youngest sister and had become a widow long ago. This did not seem to have impacted on her life very much. Departed husband was rarely mentioned. Bertie, her son who lived with her was a solicitor and led a very separate life. He might appear on Saturday afternoons with a box of groceries and occasionally stay for tea before giving me a lift home en route to his club. Aunty Victoria was an eccentric free spirit though a little hampered by ill health. She cooked many middle eastern delicacies and on Saturday afternoon she entertained an eclectic bunch of loners including me. In the summer she had her daughter and grandchildren, who were a similar age to myself, up from London and we played table tennis incessantly in her attic. She found much in her life to laugh at and her house oozed character full of goodies from Egypt, antiques, silver and spider plants. She also had a very large early model television set and I would arrive before the other guests and sit mesmerised in front of it. Other members of the family joined us for Saturday tea from time to time. Once cleared up, we got out the cards and ran the gamut of card games for up to 6 people until home time at 9.0pm.

Sometimes I got to stay over at Rosemary's house and I was initiated into a club that she and the 'old' girls had started some time before. Our job was to write plays though we never did perform. Both my best friends had parents from other countries. Anne's family were Polish and she told me how her father only escaped with his life when the German in charge tipped him off to run before the other prisoners were shot. Rosemary's father was a refugee from Austria. I was becoming acutely aware of injustice and wickedness and read books on the brutality of the Russian regime which allowed me to make black and white statements about right and wrong. Rosemary's Quaker mother looked a little quizzical at times. She was also vegetarian and I was always surprised that they were able to survive and find enough to eat.

When I was 12, my father took me away to Southport by myself. I had set myself an allowance of so many pennies a day to play on the slot machines and in general had a wonderful seaside time. But when I got back my mother had discovered a lump in her breast and her failing health and cancer treatments were a backcloth to family life from then on. Possibly because of time running out when I was 14, we went on our first Thomas Cook holiday abroad – two weeks to Austria in September. I was enchanted from the flight to the fields of wild flowers, the mountains, the painted Tyrolean houses, the thick feather duvets and the balconies. There is a happy photo of us dining out at a Tyrolean evening. For the second week we were joined by Guy (of the hotel 7 years earlier) and his mother. The September sun shone on us. The only downer was my lack of clothes. My only summer dress was my school uniform and I was beginning to feel distinctly unattractive as I became aware of the gorgeous young man who was our tour guide for the day out in Salzburg.

Sure enough, that summer was to be my mother's last. She got weaker and yellower as the autumn wore on. My father bought her a gramophone so that she could listen to her favourite music. My brother was farmed out to various supportive friends. Relations came and went. I think I chose to believe that she would get better but the cancer had got to her liver and there was nothing to do but make her comfortable. She and her doctor agreed when the end was to be. There was an evening when I, busy as usual, was getting ready to go out to a performance of Macbeth. Two days earlier my father had taken me aside to tell me that she was definitely dying. This evening he asked me to say goodbye to her. She gave me a look I shall never forget of love and farewell though I didn't know or appreciate it at the time. I blamed myself for some years that I had not reciprocated that look or properly said goodbye because when I returned from the play, she was breathing in a very strange and noisy way. I later learned that the doctor had been and administered something to send her on her way. She died in the early hours of the morning.

In some ways not much changed. I marvelled that I could still be at school doing lessons and my mother had died .But that is what happened. I continued to amass status and badges in the Girl Guides. I continued to go on and lead Youth hostel expeditions in Derbyshire. My father employed one au pair after another. I went youth hostelling with a few school friends in the winter half term a few month's after my mother's death and came back to find a 'For sale' notice in front of the house. My father had been posted at short notice to London. Off he went with my brother to stay with an old school friend of his in Streatham whilst I went to stay with my aunt and grandfather back in North Manchester. It was a long commute to school and not always easy to fit in my homework – now approaching GCE exam time. By this time I knew Macbeth off by heart and could produce the relevant quotes to score well in the Literature paper. My father, meanwhile, had found a house to buy in Sevenoaks and made arrangements for my brother to attend the local primary school and for me to attend the sixth form of the girls secondary the following year. I was getting used to starting afresh. Yet leaving my school friends with whom I had shared some six years of my life was a difficult wrench.

Sevenoaks Age 16–18

Walthamstow Hall – a school for the daughters of missionaries. Here there were boarders and dens and a different culture to get used to. I was in the South, a commuter belt for London which was a different world from the industrial smoggy suburbs of Manchester. I was disappointed my father chose a house which was a modern box on the edge of the town instead of a nineteenth century house which nestled behind a green near the centre. I gradually became part of a foursome which mocked the etiquette we were being taught as young ladies. School dinner was the most ritualised. We were assigned to tables of some 10 pupils of which only one was in our class. In this way it was thought we would develop the art of polite conversation and get to know, and be known, throughout the school. Each table in turn was required to sit on the top table with the Headmistress. She was an elegant, warm person who genuinely wanted the best for us and to know us I think. She had photos of past pupils in her study/sitting room and she told us of her Welsh holiday cottage where she spent all her holidays usually in the company of other members of staff. Yet there was a grand canyon of a gap between us and the tragedy was that she never could get to know us in anything but our roles. She asked me if I liked my last school and when I said 'Yes' she said she was 'So pleased.'

I had English, History and Latin lessons with two teachers for each subject. As well as this I was in a small group of 'S' level students. We were preparing for possible entry to Oxbridge – one student went there after staying on part of a third year. The main advantage of this group was that we embarked on autonomous projects. Hence I could go to the local library in my free periods to look at archival material relating to the part of Sevenoaks where I lived – the Bradbourne estate. I also embarked on a study of Hitler and 'Mein Kampf'. We were certainly encouraged by our teachers-formidable and devoted in their own way-to think independently, have our own opinions, and make our own lives. In this environment I flourished to a large extent. However, there were awkward adolescent sexual underminings. Some girls already had steady boyfriends but my group did not. Indeed it was a strategic quandary as to how to access the boys' school if you did not have a convenient way in such as a brother, or friends of parents with sons. The one point of official contact was the school dance. We four embarked on a blind date scheme where we wrote inviting four unknown boys to join us. Amazingly the most attractive one – name forgotten - paired up with me and started to walk me home and gave me my first kiss. In my confusion I said it would be better if I finished the walk home alone - what would my father think?! I was left bereft not knowing how to make contact again and thinking that I ought not to though I desperately wanted to. There were one or two meetings with other boys that year though I didn't fancy them in the way I had the first one.

When I was away at a Rangers (senior girl guide) camp, my beloved grandfather died. It was a relatively quick death they said. He got pneumonia and died six weeks later. My father did not know how to cope with my grief. I was angry that no-one had told me he might be dying and that I had not been invited to go and see him.

In the school holidays I and my group were keen to make money. I started at a local Findus factory on a conveyor belt packing braised beef in gravy. A boy my age started also and I noted that his pay was higher than mine. Why? Another summer I worked in the hop fields where there were also commercial blackberries which I picked. The hop pickers from East London lived in temporary huts and their way of life was an eye-opener. I remember asking a young girl if she was looking after her brother. She indignantly put me straight- the baby was hers. One Christmas I was at last allowed and able to get a job in London at Selfridges. I was in an antiquated office way above the store filing receipts. But the last summer holiday I was at home paid for by my father to look after my brother. This was a chore and a form of imprisonment. No matter: I was about to escape.

In the last year at school I got my university place at Sussex. I also was accepted to go on Voluntary Service Overseas to Nigeria. This combined with being elected as a prefect (the whole school cast votes) gave me status and meant that I left school on a high with some confidence. Future possibilities blurred the disappointment of the conundrums about how to relate to the opposite sex. I also looked forward to moving away from my family and to leaving what had become a cloying environment – the middle class white commuter belt of Sevenoaks.

I was launched into a year of adventure and somehow knew from the time I got my plane ticket that this was going to be one of the best.

2

Nigeria 1963-4 (looking back)

Delayed by a bout of mumps I set off on my adventure to do a year's teaching in an Anglican Girls' boarding school in Western Nigeria. For many years I would look back and refer to it as The 'Best Year in my life' though when I read letters to my father – a sort of diary substitute – it seems a good time certainly, but not quite the best. These are extracts from the letters chosen as a 68 year old looks back on her 18 year old self.

I have to imagine before this era of globalisation how far away Nigeria seemed. Most travel there was by sea on the Elder Dempster line. It took a fortnight. However, I travelled by air. I tried to return by sea but opted out when potential travelling companions did not materialise. Dropping out 'because I would have to be a fortnight on my own' seems particularly strange given the, to me now, hair-raising adventures I undertook when I was there. I am amused by some of the dated language- 'super' 'damned' 'dratted'. And reminded of the easy acquisition of local terms-

'chop' (meal), 'bathday' (birthday) etc. It seemed I felt at home very quickly. Far more difficult was the return to the UK, with a quick trip to Sevenoaks where my father lived, and a few weeks later to my new life at Sussex University.

Long before the era of computers, letter writing, and (equally important) letter receiving, was essential in keeping up links with school friends, relations and family. The importance of keeping a diary for the future –now?- was impressed upon me and in writing to my father I quite openly aim for this to be kept safe 'as I haven't had time to write the diary'. A Christmas present of a blank page-a-day diary arrived from Nellie in February. It had come via my father where it had arrived for Christmas. Nellie was a char lady who had worked for the family in 1951-2 when we lived in Kendal. She faithfully sent me a weekly copy of 'The Eagle' all through my teens. Regrettably I lost contact with her soon after my return to the UK. I thus have a mundane daily record of what happened from February–September 1964 as well as– at times – novelesque letters.

I have no recollection of some of the events mentioned and many of the people I met or stayed with on my travels. Frustrating. I write of a particularly adventurous trip to the Cameroons –

‘We stayed wherever we could’- well where did we stay?

On the other hand I have some striking images that arc not touched on at all. Miss Moss, the Principal with whom I lived, and myself at 9.00pm would do a round of the compound using our Tilley lamps to avoid the coiled snakes basking in the moonlight. The kitchen, with a stale smell of cockroaches, housed the food cupboard on legs in tins of water to keep off the ants, the water filter-- a great ceramic pot in two halves, and the charcoal iron. I also remember feeling sexually adrift, drawn to Jerry, an American teacher who called quite often and taught at the nearby boy’s establishment. I could not but be envious of my friend 60 miles away who had some kind of relationship with Herb, an American Peace Corps volunteer (PCV). At our induction weekend ,it had been clearly stated that it would be unwise to have transient relationships.

I notice some endearing characteristics I had and still have – a tendency to leap in unaware of the depth of the task to be: and some not so endearing ones – a tendency to pomposity and being opinionated.

So I picture myself in all my innocence revelling in the challenges of being a teacher, running a dispensary, organising sports events, meeting Nigerian dignitaries, being invited to meet British Council ones, and living in a dynamic affectionate community of young girls, some older than myself, with adventurous travels all over expecting to be put up and welcomed by any and every expat -- especially other VSO's or PCV's. I marvel at the fearlessness of that young woman.

There is no doubt that the experience had a profound influence on the rest of my life. It changed my course of study from Sociology to African History. It endeared me to teaching. It showed me that there were other kinds of arrangements for bringing up children especially where the women were dominant. It made me want to repeat the experience, but in this I was doomed. By the time I had finished my degree, Nigeria was in a state of civil war, and the year in Sierra Leone was in no way as great. It too descended into a bloody war not long afterwards. In an awkward way it set me apart from those contemporaries whose life experience was confined to Europe. Having a sense of what a developing country has to offer made me question what development had come to be in the West.

My edited letters to my father from September to January follow and give a flavour of the year itself which ended the following September

Getting there

Lagos Airport Hotel September 27th

This describes the journey at length on a Nigerian Airways, Boeing 707 with a window seat. There was a stop in Rome,

At this point the seat next to me (hitherto empty) was filled by a very Irish priest- very Irish and very devout- he'd just been at Lourdes for a few days and caught a chill!! He had much to talk about in between his devotions of course – he was gabbling and crossing away at a book in Latin.

Then came the desert - a fantastic spectacle- two hours flight without seeing habitation. First the sand was very red and softly rippled like the sand at the seaside that hasn't been touched by water for a long time. Then it turned to smooth ripples covered with dark patches – the reflections of wispy clouds. The clouds passed and there was not a sign of a cloud either in the 35,000 feet below or the other thousands of feet above – just a solitary moon in the parched sky

landing at Kano

I saw between the green orchard-like crops outside the city, compounds of mushroom huts – masses and masses of them…

And then to a night in Lagos waiting to catch the plane to Benin the next day where I was met by the British Council and the bursar from the school in the school car which drove me to St, Catherine's School (60 miles).

5th October 1963

Dear Pa

Happy birthday of the 1st. I'm sorry this wish is rather belated and the present will be even more belated. Today is Sat. am and the only day I shall be free to go shopping. I planned to explore Owo by myself but unfortunately the rainy season which ought to have been over is giving forth. Miss Moss and I started off in the car at 7.45am along the mud track which leads to the main road – the track was a raging torrent and after about ¼ of an hour the car stuck. I tore up the road fully clad in galoshes, umbrella and mac to Michael's house – Michael being the driver. He came down and Miss Moss gave him detailed instructions as to how to get the car out and then we waded back the way we had come so no shopping this morning Im afraid…..

I have now been at St. Caths a week and feel as if I have been here a hundred years – There is very little Westernisatiion and conditions are very different from Sevenoaks but still human nature is the same and I feel quite accustomed to my situation.

My first view of St.Caths. was the sign 'Visiting on Saturdays only 5-6pm'which seemed rather prison-like but this applies to boyfriends only and parents roll up at any time.

I am staying with Miss Moss. She has a bungalow and I've got a large spacious room at the front. Miss Moss is approx 60 (56 actually) very thin, extremely kind and fairly liberal in her views – I get on with her fine. The school has six classes, and is 180 strong. Class 6 are taking the Cambridge Overseas Certificate for the first time next month. I am in charge of P.E. for the school, Health Science through the school and English Class1. P.E. is very popular. I take a class first period in the morning and also one class after school at 5.00pm per day. There is one netball court and one tennis quoit court and 30 girls in the vicinity of them all at the same time is extremely hectic – it's a lung match more than anything else. After each session I return to the house dripping with sweat and dive for my sore throat tablets. The girls are so keen that they spent a great deal of time yesterday cutting the grass. Cutting grass is usually a punishment so I was rather surprised….

English is very easy to teach but Health Science!! Class 1 and class 6 have got textbooks but none of the other classes have. All I can do is teach the other classes out of class 6's text book. It was absolute hell last week – reading up all the work by paraffin lamp at night and trotting out some rather dull facts to one bored class after another. I had hoped to get to Owo to try and buy some books myself today….

I get up at 6.am , breakfast 7am, 7.40 dispensary,7.55 assembly to which none of the other staff go except me – hypocrite that I am- 8.20 games and so on until 2.pm – exhausted read up Health Science, 9pm bed. It gets dark about 6.30pm here and I retire to jeans and long sleeved shirt – mosquito protection.

The flies are not too bad – no worse than Switzerland in fact and the climate is cool especially when it rains.

Tues. was Republic Day. All the schools march past the head Chief and the best school gets an award. St C's was second. It is the largest girls' school in the vicinity. I returned to the town to watch dancing billed to start at 3pm – it eventually began at 4.30pm. Miss Moss left me there as she had some work to do and anyway I was keen to walk home by myself.

I met a Mrs B there. She teaches at Imade, the Boy's school and is one of the wives of Justus A – Mr P's friend (*Mr P was the father of a school friend and Justus had been one of his students and hence a contact made in advance*). Mrs B who has been made a Chief introduced me to all the other Chief s but unfortunately the Ilowo, the head Chief was away as he had gone to the Republic celebrations in Ibadan.

I was very slow walking back as a European on foot is an unusual sight and everybody saw fit to greet me – quite the opposite from Sevenoaks. In these circumstances I was rather glad to get a lift back – a Lancs man who works at the trade centre here.

The girls are very keen to work and the older ones have far more responsibility than their English counterparts. The boarding side of the school is run entirely by the girls themselves as the Nigerian teachers take no part and Miss Moss has quite enough to do already. The girls in the classes are all ages – some of them don't know their ages at all but those in the top class must be at least 20. The staff, some of whom are graduates, are the educated elite. They employ the girls to do all their work- quite often they don't go to classes and never until quite a time has elapsed after the bell. Miss Moss finds it very difficult to cope with them but so far I have found them fairly friendly…..

The main difficulty of the school is money. The fees inclusive of board and uniform are £60 per annum and they don't come in. Frequently Miss Moss has to send the girls home until they pay their fees, There is a government grant owing and also a council grant about £1,500 in all I believe. The last Principal called in one day for the first time since she left on the verge of a nervous breakdown three years ago. She is young and very lively and is teaching in Eastern Nigeria. She has another VSO whom I met on the Sevenoaks course with her and invited me to spend a week at Christmas there. After that Miss Moss is taking me up North to Kaduna and possibly Kano.

The Nigerians are very poor. Michael the driver gets £7.10 a month and lots of that goes on income tax+ 8s National Provident. He has a wife, wife's sister and children to support. Joseph the nightwatchman gets £3.10s a month and has no other employment. I don't know how much John our housekeeper gets.

The Peace Corps volunteers – a married couple of 22 haven't come yet because the husband has a blood disease and is in hospital and there is no indication when they will come.

Having gone through the initial set up of the different routines I doubt if the rest of the year will be any different so there won't be much to write in future,……

12th October 1963

…. Up to yesterday the week was very routine. Health Science coming a bit easier.. although without reference books and the knowledge it is a bit of a strain… I was doing the skeletal system with class V and in order to do it borrowed Class V1 notes and trotted them out to to V. With class IV I've just finished a fairly interesting course on the history of the conquest of disease and have set them a two week project – a biography of one of the personalities connected with this topic. Class 111 are wilting under my explanation – rather confused I fear – of the blood system. This is easier for me however as I did something on this in the third year at W.G.S. Class 11 have spent all the time on'the eye'. This happens to be the only thing I know since I did it in Physics and I was tempted to spend rather longer time on it than I ought.

Yesterday we had the shock of our lives when a white couple knocked at our door – the Peace Corps Volunteers and not expected till January. Poor things – their house was not at all ready –filthy in fact and no equipment. They are very sweet about 22 years old and only married a month ago. (They had only known each other 6 weeks having met on the Peace Corps induction course). Gary Petersen is luckily trained in Biology and is going to relieve me of classes V and V1 although his main work is at Imade Boys School. Angela is going to take some of everybody's periods and I am down to 19 per week – luxury! I am helping with the choir. In 3 weeks time I am taking the choir to Ibadan for a broadcast but they haven't got the book of songs they're to sing yet.

I'm hoping to improvise a tennis court soon – there is some hope of the school buying tennis rackets if the ground is cleared but there still remains the problem of a net…..

No – I'm not homesick although perhaps I will find the work dull when I settle into a routine. By the way I'm taking geography next term so I'll be fully educated by the end of the year as geography and Biology were the two subjects I couldn't take at 'O'level!....

18th October

Nothing spectacular on the compound this week – have graduated from the Conquest of Disease to Public health water supply and from the eye to the ear and from the blood system to tetanus and that's about all…

Last Sunday Alfred O (a Nigerian I met in UK) came quite unexpectedly at about 3pm. It was rather awkward as the one sacred hour of the day is 2.30-3.30 when Miss Moss has her siesta – the house is locked, the shutters closed and all visitors ignored. By chance I hadn't bothered to go for siesta and so was up to answer the door but all the same it was difficult inviting him in when I knew the noise would disturb Miss Moss… He had travelled up from Lagos arriving Owo 2am and was going back the 278 miles that evening...

The British Council in Ibadan produced a welcoming letter this week and said they would provide a bed anytime so am going to make use of it on the 9th – the choir's appearance on television…

The Petersen's are still settling in: their fridge doesn't work properly and they are still minus furnishings. I haven't been up there very much at all. Of course the Peace Corps have provided them with many things – the science kit is typical. Apart from some chemicals there is a large quantity of wood with different sizes of holes carefully drilled at intervals – these-come listed as – '8 blocks of wood with 1/8 holes' . Gary couldn't think what to do with them short of making a bird table. They've been presented with a wonderful collection of brand new paperbacks – about 200 I should think in a papier maché bookcase.

The rainy season must be almost over now… I've got through 2 Agatha Christies this week and am now onto Howard Spring 'My Son, My son 'interspersed with Kellet's 'A Short History of Religion'…..

25th October

Many thanks for the newspaper cutting.. as there is no wireless I'm completely cut off from any news. I was extremely surprised when I glanced at the paper last Sunday to see on the back a reference to the doings of Lord Home the British Prime Minister… when did MacMillan give up and why?.....

Please could you send out my french books. As Angela Petersen is a French graduate and Miss Moss considers I am a qualified French teacher, the school syllabus is changing over from Latin to French in January. January is the beginning of the school year out here. The new class 1 will take French and possibly the present class I. I think this is a great pity in some ways as the Latin is very useful when teaching English. I can often explain a point in English by going back to the Latin. On the other hand most of the surrounding countries are French speaking.

A lot of my time this week has been taken up with choir. … the Ibadan broadcast is getting very near now. I accompany all the songs except one on the organ – unfortunately this machine broke down on Weds.- the dratted C# stuck and this means whatever I play is drowned by a discordant C# so I gave up playing in the end and we just have to sing without music. To cap all, Mrs O the choir mistress was not at all well and I had to take the practices myself. I also took a music lesson. Mrs O asked me to teach one of her classes an English song.. the lesson was rather chaotic as I was lost without the organ and incapable of singing the notes myself. Fortunately some of the girls knew the song – The Wraggle Taggle Gipsies O – and they were able to carry the rest of the class along. The Yorubas have a great sense of drama – I have noticed it many times – for example when I dictated the words of the Wraggle Taggle gypsies there was a great moan when the heroine of the song renounces her lord and says

'Tonight I shall sleep in a cold open field'etc.

This is the end of the song but several of the girls came up to me and demanded to know if she went back to her lord!

Class 111's response to lessons on diseases is as dramatic. I started off with tetanus and the life of the bacteria from the horse's intestine., through the nervous system to the muscles. This results in spasms etc and finally death. On this note there was a great sigh. Likewise on the death of a patient suffering from rabies, snake bits and other tropical delicacies.

This week was varied by a staff meeting at which the staff took it upon themselves to air their grievances! Miss Moss cut this short by standing up and saying a prayer and we went back to our lessons!

I've finished off ,'My Son, My Son' and also read a paperback called 'The African' lent to me by the Peace Corps and quite readable but not very well written. My book is on the verge of being started – at least I've decided on a title 'Oyibo!' This means white skin. Whenever I go into Owo the children wave and cry and many of them come up and touch me, I am beginning to regard my white skin as a rarity myself.

I am suffering from bites dreadfully .. I had 12 bites throbbing last night ..

We had a wonderful deluge the day before yesterday – it was in the middle of my rabies lesson. The noise of the rain was deafening and I gave up trying to teach and wrote everything on the board.

Next weekend Miss Moss and I are going over to Miss Moss's sister at Iwo –

near Ibadan We are going on the Friday at half term. On the Thursday I am also going to Benin with the Petersons…

!st November'63

I am writing from Miss Moss's sister's house in Iwo near Ibadan. We came down 140 miles today. There is electric light here and millions of mosquitoes – I just walked round the house at about 5.30pm when it was still quite light and I had to come in again as I caught about 12 mosquitoes on my legs and although I bashed them they had already drawn blood. Generally they are too quick to be caught. Tomorrow we are going into shop in Ibadan.

Tues was rather a fiasco. At 8.45am Miss Moss received a note from the Ilowo that Akitola , Premier of the Western region was passing through at 8.30. This meant all the girls had to go to the main road and line it as this is always done when anyone important is around. Great excitement. At the end of games lesson, I rushed back to the house to get changed and then arrived up at the office to supervise a marching start. By this time a note had come delaying operations till 11.20am. Miss Moss and I did not go up until about 11.20 and there we found the girls wilting in the sun and no sign of any politicians. At 12.30, Miss Moss and self went back for lunch and risked missing the premier – we returned to the road about 1.pm. Finally at 1.15 Miss Moss told all the girls to return unless they particularly wanted to stay – about 6 did. After a further half an hour Angela Petersen and I cut our losses and left too. We heard later that Akintola drove by only 10mins after we left! *(description of trip to Benin with the Petersens*).

The choir broadcast for next week is suffering setbacks, There is no accommodation for the girls in Ibadan. . The tuner came yesterday, opened the organ up and was met by the massed force of cockroaches and a lizard. He put the C# right very quickly. He is the sole possessor of a piano in Owo – as he put it the inhabitants of Owo buy wives whenever they have any money but he has saved up for a piano….

7th November 1963

Dear Pa,……..

(*a visit from Miss Moss's sister)*

'Her negotiations for selling her blue car are highly amusing. She maintains that as she has looked after the car well and improved it with gadgets etc it is now worth more than the price she paid for it secondhand in June! There is a 22 year old American boy out here who was interested in buying it and she wanted over £400 for it. He refused point blank and has since got a pretty good Fiat for £240. Last week she enticed a Nigerian into buying it for £420 but he hasn't produced any cash yet. All that is by the way but with Miss Moss'sister around I daren't touch the car. She refuses to let Michael even drive it when she is around. Last weekend was absolutely hilarious with Michael sitting in state in the back of the car and Miss M's sister driving. Miss Moss's sister is quite a character and interferes with everything and has loud penetrating tones that grind into your ears. Fortunately it is very easy to find her just an absolute scream. Miss Moss who is the opposite meekly acquiesces when her sister is around and with difficulty I do too. Last weekend she was dogmatically telling me the English university entrance requirements in terms of School Certificate and Higher. I started off trying to correct or rather modernise her but soon gave up.

... The girls are indeed great characters – there is one in the youngest class who prides herself on keeping the class in order! One day, when my lesson was drowned by hilarity next door, she calmly walked out without a word and asked Mr Johnson to conduct his lesson more quietly. She also informed me quite sincerely that she thought it would be too difficult for me to all the year's work in the examination and therefore I had better set them an exam on this term's work alone. By the way that is what I am busy with at the moment – making up questions for the December end of school year examinations

(The earlier part of the letter was taken up with a discussion of what had arrived, money and practical things, part of the later part is concerned with my father's remarriage plans- what gift I should buy for them etc).

School is back to normal after last weekend although the numbers are depleted by about 30 who are not being allowed back until they have paid their fees. The Petersens have arranged to play tennis with the Ilowo (the local Nigerian chief). I haven't had an opportunity of seeing him at all. We still haven't got accommodation for the choir after the broadcast on sat. evening. The telephone lines are a dead loss – you have to book a call several hours before using it – consequently as a last resort, Miss Moss sent Mrs Olowoyo – the choir mistress – to Ibadan to try and find accommodation. She is due back today and if unsuccessful the whole trip will have to be cancelled.

Ibadan by the way is a large town with the usual stall-type shops but with department stores as well. I was quite amazed to see white people around the place – they are such a rarity here. We did not have much time in Ibadan as Mis M's sister is a late riser and the shops shut 1.30pm instead of 2pm on Sat…..

17th November 1963 *--the television broadcast and journey to Ibadan*)

Am labouring under a cloud of letters to reply to at the moment plus there seems plenty to do here…

My weekend at Ibadan was more than I had bargained for… we hired a lorry from a neighbouring school or as the Nigerians call it, a truck – it was a done-up mammy wagon. The choir of 18 piled in the back and Miss A – a Nigerian mistress – sat in uncomfortable state with me in the front with Michael. The gears were 2/3 over from the driver's side and thus we had the choice of the gears and a dig in the knee every time the gear was changed or the door side which had a large number of projections. I had the projections going and the gears coming back.

After 60 miles the brakes went wrong and we had to stop for half an hour to repair them a Ilesha. A couple of miles further on the windscreen exploded into smithereens – an oncoming car had flung up a stone. We stopped to pull all the glass out. Thereafter it was a trifle draughty.

We eventually got to Ibadan at 2pm, an hour before we were due at the television studios for a rehearsal. Ibadan grammar school for Boys but with one Girl's house had agreed to put us up – however – when we drove in there was no sign of anybody about and we had to knock several people out of siesta before we could snatch a meal and wash ourselves and the girls. It was while we were waiting that I saw my first snake – a small innocuous looking green thing hanging out of a tree. I watched its antics with amusement but was hauled back violently as it was deeply poisonous. Somewhat the worse for wear we got ourselves to the studio at 4.pm – an hour late but this did not appear to matter. The studio was occupied by brown uniforms – I realised to my horror that the organisers had made a glorious mistake and had commissioned two schools to come on the same day. At this juncture Miss A went shopping and left me to cope. We had to amalgamate the programmes. The great event took place at 6.30pm by which time the girls were limp and smitten with headaches. I was expected to accompany them though I had understood that the accompanists were supplied by the studio – I managed to get away with the accompaniment of only one song. The rest of the time I wandered about in front of the choir trying to conduct, keep the dear little things in time and dissuade them from looking as if the H bomb was about to fall. Chaos reigned utterly even to my receiving a message to omit the repeat of the last song because of lack of time and then some mechanic roaring 'repeat'..

When I came out of the performance Miss A was standing in the hall being crouched over by an amorous guitarist. On the way back to the school she announced that she wanted to be dropped in town as she was going out that night and that I would see to the girls! I was somewhat aghast but actually the girls behaved perfectly and there was never a moment's trouble with them.

Miss A and I were staying in a guest chalet but having our meals with a Miss Langa – one of the female staff of the school. I have never met anyone more easy to talk to than Miss Langa – she is a black South African and was really very kind to me. I think it was the first time I realised that colour of skin really makes no difference whatsoever. She used to be Principal of a school in Ondo and had a VSO there last year – however she found the problems – staff, financial too great and gave up. I had the evening meal with her and then she asked how I would like to go out to a night club! I leapt at the suggestion

– partly as I thought I would get my own back on Miss A!!

Miss A came back at 9pm and the girls went to bed at 9.30pm. Miss Langa and friend called for me at 10.pm and I got back about 1.30am. Friend – can't remember his name took us to the Lafia Night club – this is the most exclusive Club in Ibadan and I'm afraid I wasn't at all dressed for it. The patrons were a mixed crew – and the Whites – dreadful – I felt quite ashamed of the colour of my skin – mostly spinsters around 40 waiting to be picked up plus some rather gruesome – looking business men one of whom came up and asked me in smarmy tones if my escort could spare me for the next number – I assured him, he could not! The rage here is Highlife – a shuffling kind of step but a little more interesting than the twist.

The next day we set off early and on the way back we passed a mammy wagon accident. I think we might have been the first on the scene. I didn't realise it was an accident at first – I noticed people sitting down outside a mammy wagon with their baskets of cocoa beans and thought they were just resting. It was only when we got near that I heard wailing and saw that the figures were not just sitting but were covered in streams of blood. Michael drove on and on and would not stop until he had put about 2 miles between us and the accident. Finally he did stop and we debated what to do – it was a difficult situation. I didn't fancy having 18 hysterical girls on my hands and favoured dropping the younger girls at the next village and then going back to pick up as many of the people that could be moved as possible

It was rather cowardly I suppose but we decided to leave it – we stopped a car which was going in the direction of a hospital first though.

On Weds we had another diversion. Mrs B (Justus A's wife) called round. She was going to Oka , 27 miles away the next day and wondered if I would like the drive. As I only had knitting with class V that afternoon, Miss M let me go. It was a most attractive journey – the first time I have seen any views or mountains here at all – the road to Ibadan is hemmed in by forest all the way.

On the way back we stopped at a Catholic school to leave a message. We were welcomed with open arms by two Irish boys who had been there 2 and 6 weeks respectively. Apparently life there is very grim. Oka is on a mud track, 20 miles from the nearest road – it really was a bush school and they had no car. Mrs B invited me back to a meal afterwards as she put it –

she thought it her duty to take me around after Mr P (my school friends father) had sent a letter, While I was there Justus called + the Petersens + the American, Jerry, so it was quite a gathering. However Maggie B was rather dozy as she is undergoing a strong antibiotic treatment for boils.

Apparently a European Club opened in Owo that evening. It is in a very convenient place for me – at the corner of St. C's road and the main road about 10 mins walk away. The Petersens have been going there a bit but I don't fancy going there by myself and Miss M has no time. We might join in the holidays. Since there are only about 12 Europeans in Owo I can't see the membership expanding very much.

This weekend I have been very lazy. Miss M's sister came up and like a fool I didn't keep my trap shut and found myself carried away on the usual theme of university entrance. Really Miss M's sister knew very little about the subject and rather infuriated me by upholding London as the best university in GB. I got a letter from the Nigerian to whom Miss M's sister sold her car.

'I think you are really nice.. I was told you belonged to the V.S.O.. I am happy to find youths like you volunteering to serve less privileged persons'.

…. I am also in charge of the school uniform. This entails distributing 144 PE blouses that have just come from the dressmakers for 173 girls. It also entails making uniform lists for next year. My dispensary minion has just been made a prefect – a disaster since this means she can no longer carry on with the dispensary. I shall now have to put an active oar in it…

Three staff are leaving at the end of term… I shall be fourth senior mistress then. Miss M is trying to get another Peace Corps.

It doesn't look as though I shall be able to start anything original as so much needs seeing to of the existing structure. In Jan I hope to revive the Debating society

Beaver, the bush dog here had three puppies about a fortnight ago. They came out of the bush for the first time this weekend but they are still very shy. Miss Moss is not sure what to do with them – 2 of the last batch got eaten.

Class V1 is going to leave right after the exams. One girl goes to take up nursing at Redhill. She is extremely pleasant I though I would give her your address…

19th November

I could write volumes about the members of staff – in fact the last Principal did when she handed the ropes to Miss

Moss – it makes very amusing reading....Miss Moss has decided she had better burn the book when she leaves (*I then proceed to write a not very complimentary account of staff members*). Apart from the teaching staff there is matron – old, very sweet and simple, 4 compound workers, 3 cooks, Rubin, cook, Michael, 2 night watchmen, Ezekiel the carpenter plus two apprentices – all of these are extremely courteous and have a misplaced respect for white skins in general.

30th November

.. the main news is exams- the West African cert. exams finish next Tues. and Class V1 are then disappearing The girls seem to have taken it fairly well - at least we haven't had any incidents- at Imade one boy walked out of the chemistry exam, went off his head and smashed up the Principal's office.

During the exams I have introduced a P.E. variation – the usual netball is far too noisy for exam conditions – I have taken the girls at scouts pace up the mud track to the junction, had a few team games on a piece of ground and then walked them back. This was quite popular with the younger forms but the older ones were not too keen as you can imagine.

School exams were to start on Weds .a fortnight before the end of term but there's a rumour that the government are shortening the term to end on the 13th – a practice they have out here and on the strength of that Miss M decided to start the exams on Monday. This put me in a proper panic. I hadn't finished all my question papers and had promised certain classes revision on Mon. and Tues. Anyway I got them all done last night – the bursar used 500 sheets rolling them off and was rather exhausted by the effort! Next week will be ing and then reports. I'm really looking forward to the holidays and then I'm going away a lot of the time. I shall have to put in health Science swotting too as I'm doomed to take Class V in preparations for West African Certificate next term.

Everybody here was very shocked at the death of Kennedy - he has a great name here principally because of the 5000 Peace Corps in the country. The Petersens managed to get Voice of America on their set and we heard a description of the laying in state.

On Weds. there was a Red Cross bazaar and Angela was asked to open it. I promised to go and walked down with some girls who were to be presented with certificates. Unfortunately it was an absolute fiasco.... on account of (my view) the high charges which meant the girls were unable to buy anything).

Christie the new head girl walked down with me, was very pleasant and invited me to stay at her house in Benin. There's great commotion here about Cherabim and Seraphim. The three house mistresses and Matron have just come down to the house with stories of the said sect – apparently Christie is the ringleader and organises devotional meetings, involving shakings, visions, the lot. Another unfortunate aspect is that they consider themselves clean as opposed to the nonparticipants. Naturally enough the staff want it stamped out in the school. I'm not quite sure how Miss Moss proposes to deal with the situation.

I take it your marriage is still fixed to for the 20th.

New Year

2nd Jan 1964

Many thanks for your letter which I received after travelling..

My monthly salary of £5 has been paid up fine as have all the staff salaries – out of Miss Moss' pocket. Walter P, the bank manager advised her not to do this and I thought it was very risky. At any rate it has worked out allright now as the government has produced the grant minus about £900 which we haven't much hope of ever getting. I am feeling rather poor at the moment after holidays etc. .. Miss Moss wanted me to take £7 extra for Christmas – a fortnight's board as I was away but fortunately I managed to persuade her to keep it. It really was very sweet of her but she pays a lot extra as it is and is entirely paying for my holiday with her at Kaduna. We are staying there 12–19th. I've no idea what it will cost her but since she believes in comfort I daresay it will be very expensive.

You inquire about weather. Its very comfortable at the moment – cool and breezy – Harmattan weather. It is the equivalent of Winter – most of the leaves have fallen. The Nigerians find it too cold– it is the time when the most deaths among the Nigerians occur. From now on it gets hotter and hotter working up to a crescendo in April I understand…

Originally I was to travel with a friend of Miss U's as far as Asaba… about 160 miles from Owo on the Niger. At Asaba stay with a VSO and travel with her to Ibiaku, a village 40 miles further on near Ikot Ekpene. Well the night before I was to start I got a letter from Gwynne U saying the lift had fallen through but she would be glad to have me if I could get there for Christmas. I also got a telegram from the VSO at Asaba saying she was spending

Christmas at Oyo near Ibadan. You can imagine I felt rather glum and decided to abandon the project but my only alternative was to stay in the house by myself as Miss Moss had arranged to go to Lagos with her sister. In the end I decided to try to get to Ibiaku by public transport I'm jolly glad I did as it was a great experience.

There are various modes of transport her and none of them particularly safe except for Armels. Armels runs actual coaches and also mail lorries – cattle truck affairs containing mail and passengers that really look rather grim. Apart from Armels there are mammy wagons, then there are taxis – private taxis operating on a local scale mostly mini-minors and also public taxis – Peugot estate cars that hold 7 people. Well I made a few inquiries about public transport and owing to the tendency around here to call anything from a taxi to a mammy wagon, a bus , I waited outside the post office from 9–11.15 for an Armels coach. It wasn't long before I realised my mistake that the one coach only passes through Owo per day at 4pm and that the vehicle due to arrive at 9.00am was a mail lorry. Mr Johnson being the good-natured soul that he was waited with me, and secured me a seat. I could never have managed without him – the lorry was absolutely cram full. It had come from

Lagos and consequently could only take one more passenger. The journey was surprisingly comfortable. Of course I got the usual stares. I was a little put out when we drew to a halt only 15miles out of Owo as the bridge was down. I asked someone how long we were likely to delay and was cheerfully informed that we might not get on until the next day. By some stroke of luck which seems to have been with me all through my travels we managed to cross the bridge minus a few planks after only a 20 min wait.

I got to Asaba about 6pm. The driver was wonderful, although he was behind time and in danger of missing the last ferry over the Niger. He put me down by the school where I was to stay the night and even got hold of a passing cyclist to carry my luggage for me. Jane B, the Principal of the school with whom I was staying was great fun– it's the school mentioned in the Daily Telegraph in connection with a VSO – you may remember the cutting about it.

Next day I crossed the Niger with Jane the present VSO at Asaba as she was going shopping in Onitsha. We crossed in a dreadful contraption which Mr Johnson had specifically warned me not to patronise but Jane said it was okay. It went under the name of 'Erico' and was a double storied launch absolutely crammed to sinking point. The officials drove herds and herds of people onto it plus animals and chickens. There is no regulation about weight apparently and of course the owners are out to make as much as they can. … I had with me a steward working in Asaba and going home to Ikot Ekpene and in return for his fare he showed me the ropes of transport in the East. We got to Aba by flying taxi– also known as flying coffin – 100 miles in 1 hr 50 mins– all for 8/6 each but there I was stranded…. I had to take a taxi for 12/– and be very diddled in the process. I had a wonderful time at Ibiaku. It was especially wonderful to see some fellow V.S.Os at last and then Gwynne U really laid on a wonderful programme for me. She took me to Calabar one day. This involved a 2 hr sail from Oron along the river Cross, contains the grave of Mary Slessor and is the most attractive Nigerian town I have seen. It's built on a slope and height is something I value after the flatness of Owo. On the Sunday Gwynne got one of her friends to drive us through the bush. This is something you can't do in the West. In the West most of the villages are on main roads, the ones that are not can only be reached by bush paths. In the E the main roads are in much better condition and there are no villages actually on the roads. The villages are all on dirt bush roads within the thick palm forests and you can drive for miles through a maze of roads. We ended up at a bush church – a Mennonite one – where we took part in the service – quite different from the Owo Anglican counterparts.

Ibiaki school has been founded since '49 and is about 300 strong, well established with no money problems, run almost entirely by expatriates. Failities are in some ways better than those at an English grammar school. I'm so glad I'm not V.S.Oing there. I just couldn't cope with being cooped up with middle aged spinsters for terms on end. As the staff are so good, Judy and Glen are looked upon as very raw juniors which I suppose VSO's are. Here where the staff aren't so good I do come in for quite a bit of responsibility. Judy is a graduate VSO and Glen an ordinary one. She is very sheltered and not allowed to travel by public transport at all. She is going for a holiday to Jos but is allowed to do so only by 1st class rail. The climate is far worse at Ibiaku– sandflies all day, scitoes by night- very humid. Altogether I think the holiday was most valuable in making me realise how lucky I am to be at Owo. The VSO's at Ibiaku are quite happy. It really is amazing how VSO HQ have managed to fit us all into appropriate projects – not like the Peace Corps I've met.

Those in towns wish they were in bush; those in bush would give anything to be in towns. The Petersens are an exception though, they are very happy here.

I came back on the 27th. I decided without much hope of succeeding to try to get to Owo all in one day. Again luck succeeded luck. I got to the government ferry at Onitsha by flying taxi without a hitch and on the ferry was a lecturer from Ibadan who offered me a lift right through to Owo. It was a lovely journey as he wanted to examine the Benin antiquities and so we looked round the museum bronzes and also went to the Afin, famous for its terra cotta sculpture. He lived in Cheadle and also knows Mr R at Ibadan who is the father of a girl at W. Hall.

When I got back I was welcomed by the compound at large as though I had been away years. All this was most flattering……

Lately I have been very idle. Sunday however was again a wonderful day. Maggie B asked me to go into the Northern region to see Chief Justus A. It was a lovely trip with quite different geographical features – some very picturesque rounded rocks.; marvellous views and no palm forest. Unfortunately when we got to Esie we found the Chief was out but Maggie took me to see what he was working on– all that involved going to see the Oba, paying him an appropriate dash and then being given a guide to the House of Images. We had to trek the last mile or so through the bush. The images were absolutely fantastic– thousands upon thousands of stone images about 2 feet high. The antiquities department found them in a heap and is now trying to piece them together and solve the question of how they came to be there. There is no stone for making the images around that region. It is not known how they were made or what they were used for. I would really like to have taken some photos but haven't got enough money for a film at the moment.

Am now compiling uniform lists. swotting up Health Science and am about to sort through a load of books which are due to arrive……

(The letters continue until and after my departure, the following September. There is another adventure to the Cameroons travelling through mangrove swamps on a little passenger ferry. The letters also convey the immense sense of loss on my dutiful return.)

3

Student 1964 –7

Glossy brochures arrive (2011) extolling the ravishing times students of all ages had and have at Sussex. Much as I accept the role of student and much as I love libraries and books, I felt then as I continue to feel that I was living out someone else's dream, that of Asa Briggs the first chancellor and the staff he brought in to found it.

At 19, I was a year older than the majority of students after the eventful year as a V.S.O. in Nigeria. That difference set me apart from most of my fellow students though a few had also had what came to be known as gap years. There were of course a sprinkling of mature students and some international students but most had come straight from British grammar and public schools.

I never warmed to the Sussex Downs which stretched on the horizon from one end of the county to Lewes nearby and then Newhaven. They seemed bleak without the wildness of the moors to be found in the North or the West. Basil Spence's architecture was good concrete and fitted into Stanmer Park but lacked the sense of inspiration of ancient buildings with learning woven into their walls. I guess they lacked a soul. The guest house where I lived had perhaps more of a seaside holiday history albeit on the saucy side. Before the Halls of residence were built we all stayed in guest houses. Mine was in a typical terrace in a narrow street in Kemp Town. It had an overflow next door where I lived on the ground floor – something of a flat with a little kitchen. I shared one room with a fellow English student with an equally German surname and the back room was occupied by a ballet dancer who was much older and grander and went out with one of the lecturers.

It was a short walk down to the sea where the long line of sea front stretching to Hove trails the town behind and creates a linear settlement. It seemed to me there was no heart or centre unless you counted the Clock Tower or the Pavilion or the station. Parallel to the sea front and at the other end of the street where we lived was a collection of run down shops and cafes.

The morning began with breakfast provided in the guest house after which we made our way into the university by bus or train. The day was spent on campus in the library, the snack bar or the refectory. If we were back by supper time we often ate at 'The Black Cat', a cheap eaterie in the back street near the guest house.

In the introductory week I learned that a new School (in older universities this would be called a Department) was being set up in African and Asian studies. This was obviously just right for me and I quickly changed from sociology and politics in the European school to History in the new school. The format for the first year for all arts students remained the same, however, and we embarked on two compulsory courses one based on Tawney's 'Religion and the Rise of Capitalism' and the other on philosophical questions such as 'What is good?' and 'Does Truth exist? There were few lectures, but emulating the Oxbridge tutorial system, teaching was essentially one to two and for each week one prepared one or two essays to be read out and discussed with a fellow student and tutor. This resulted in huge areas of unscheduled time much of which was spent in the snack bar.

How to spend time? Perhaps this is the most crucial life-long learning question of all. At that age one spent spare time finding out about one's fellow beings and making alliances.

My strategy was to create and get involved with groups or societies as they were called, (apart from the Union set who had their own public school dynamics). My main allegiance was to the Liberal and Radical society where I initiated a journal and we had speakers down besides going off to assist in national election campaigns. But I also was a founder member of the African and Asian society and Barbara Castle, the then Minister for Overseas development came to speak. In my role as Chairman I dined on steak with her at the Four Aces in the Lanes. Because Sussex had a certain kudos it was not difficult to persuade leading names of the day to make the journey down from London to speak even though at that time the university was not yet up to its full capacity.

The 60's are remembered as a time of sexual liberation and nowhere was more part of the 60's scene than Sussex. The vital question of the day in that first year among us young women was whether it was okay to lose one's virginity. News passed round as to who had done it and those of us who had not, watched to see if anything about them had changed in any subtle way. It was not until my second year that I tested the water and it was not that simple. Abortion was still illegal and I heard of one student who was unable to have children after a botched job. My doctor was dead against the pill which had recently become available. He would not give it to his own daughter he said. Having a cap fitted involved going to a private practice in Hove – not too seedy – where I was asked if I really did want to go ahead. In one way or another, the event which I had imbued with great significance was altogether a bit of a let down.

Having been to a girls' school and with a brother who was much younger than me I had had little contact with 'boys' of my own age. There was a friend from childhood but although we were clearly fond of each other we did not know how to progress to boyfriend and girlfriend though we visited each other from time to time and wrote to each other up to the time I got married. There is something sad about reflecting that bright as we were, we had no experience of how to communicate our feelings to each other so that neither of us knew how the other felt. We were both members of our respective university Humanist society and there was mention in our letters of arranging a joint event which did not in fact come off. He went on to have a successful life in academia and although my parents met his from time to time, we lost contact.

Sussex had more female than male students and the majority of the young men were on the science side. They led an entirely different life with a fully scheduled timetable and no time to consider the deeper meaning of life questions. As a whole they seemed immature and socially inept. However through the Liberal and Radical society I met two working class lads from the East end. In my fascination for learning about different lives, they had much to tell me. I also spent snack bar time with a mature Scotsman who was engaged to be married. There was something solid and safe about him. As time went on the yearning for a boyfriend became more urgent especially as it seemed the supply of available ones seemed to be in danger of drying up leaving a few hard to get and confirmed bachelors.

One of my worst memories is of the hops in Falmer house. This was a cattle et experience with girls waiting on one wall to be invited to dance. I was not a glamorous or even goodlooking catch. Humiliation was as good as it got. It was difficult for the boys too. Supposing they were rebuffed?

There was also the question of clothes. Until I made myself a mini skirt, my smartest outfit was a pale blue crimplene suit. Clothes were either for children or adults, anything inbetween did not exist.

Swinging was not my experience of the 60's

In my second year I shared a most sumptuous first floor flat in Brunswick square with a large couch to sink into, gilt framed mirror over the grand mantelpiece and polished oval table beneath a chandelier. No matter that I had a box sized room at the back overlooking a wall and virtually bereft of light. Then in my third year I turned down the possibility of another elegant flat share in Hove for a bedsit single room back in Kemp town where my boyfriend had the basement flat.

Sussex had a medical centre with a counselling service – a rare facility in those days. I did not make use of it and on reflection might have done well to. But it was seen as a place of last resort for the almost mentally ill. It was not until much later in life in my 30's that I took up counselling and appreciated how important self- absorption/knowledge was.

Had I done so earlier I might have felt more relaxed in my single status and more confident about waiting to meet the 'man of my dreams' in some more open and mature context. As it was, an accident on my Honda in my second year brought me in closer contact with one of the east end boys and after going around together during and after our courses finished we got married.

As my father said wisely but I felt inappropriately 'These things don't always last you know'.

The quality of teaching was unquestionably high and the opportunity to pursue individual ideas and research was something I valued. (In the third year I even had my own module and exam on Hindu philosophy.) My Sussex degree gave me a passport to further study and the shelter of academia was a place I returned to several times. I felt more at ease in the city universities (Bristol and Edinburgh) where you walked out into the centre of real life compared with the limitations of the campus. I was never so encouraged or tolerated as at Sussex. Later I felt hampered by petty rivalries and plain conservatism based on fears of giving offence to funding authorities. There was none of that during my time at Sussex. It was a place and a time to grow up away from the stresses and strains of the working environment and a good starting point for a radical life style.

Summer vacations

These were spent earning and travelling. The first year I accompanied my room mate who was Jewish to Israel. She had contacts in Haifa where we landed after going deck passage from Venice. Her elderly relatives were pioneers. who had come out from Germany to found a kibbutz in the 20's.There are many images from that time. I was struck first of all by the number of Mediterranean ports which were in a state of military preparedness. That was not including the Balkans– Dubrovnik and Split – which became embroiled in civil war later. Cyprus was militarised and Jerusalem was full of no go areas; the main play structure on the kibbutz was a tank and the young women we met were proud to have served in the army. Like most kibbutzes, ours was near a border and we were counselled not to go for walks on a nearby hillside. We worked on the kibbutz as olive pickers starting very early before it got too hot. There were days out too. The elderly couple doubled up to give us one of their two rooms to sleep in. They had coupons for clothes. A new coat for example could be 'bought' every 7 years. Through them we were put in contact with their daughter in Dimona, a desert town: we went to a wedding with them. Childcare was available everywhere. On the kibbutz, the children were in crèches except for one hour of family time in the evening. In Dimona there was a 24 hour nursery at the end of the street. Women were expected and needed to work. We travelled around from the Red Sea to the artistic colony of Safed, calling in at Jerusalem, the Dead Sea and other sights.

*   *   *

In the long vacation of 1966 I stayed in Brighton and moved from one basic job to another – a checker in a clothing factory, and a runner for the chef of the student refectory. I had inherited some money from Aunt Etty which bought the aforementioned Honda and a six week stay in East Africa care of an organisation called 'Experiment in International Living'. In going to Uganda, I hoped to spend a little time at Makere University in Kampala to embellish my final dissertation on the education of the Baganda elite. Uganda was a colonial invention which incorporated three Kingdoms of which the most powerful was Buganda ruled by the Kabaka who was a subject of study by my Professor.

The outward flight was delayed by two weeks which meant a prolonged wait and arriving back too late to be my cousin's bridesmaid. In the group there was, a Swiss woman, a Swedish woman, two Americans, a Scot, a Welshman and myself. We were all of a similar studenty age. We were allocated to different families in Kampala. I stayed with an Indian Sunni family who introduced me to the existence of Sunnis and Sharias. They themselves followed the teachings of the Aga Khan.

After two weeks our group reassembled and set off on a trek across Uganda to the Kenyan coast. En route we stayed in a national park containing the Murchison falls, elephants, crocodiles etc. before arriving at a Youth Hostel in Nairobi. From there we went north to Mombasa and then made for a remote village (Takauungu) near the sea where we were joined by several local Kenyan volunteers at our designated workcamp. The villagers spoke Swahili. Their faces with straight noses reflected the intermarriage of Arabs and Africans.

We slept on the floor of the one concrete building. There were two ongoing projects – one for men and one for women. The village women had almost finished theirs – a round mud hut to which we contributed by aiming mud balls on the inside to form a sort of plaster. The men were building a concrete and brick ante-natal unit to which we were diverted and laid grey blocks in straight lines mortared in by sand from the shore and concrete.

As Europeans (and Americans) we were excused the strict demarcation of male and female zones. We would never have grasped which paths winding round the palms and red mud homes we were supposed to be on. In the evenings the village women collected us and brought us to one or other or their homes where they entertained us with songs and music. Again, exceptionally, the young men in our group were allowed to accompany us.

It was a short walk down to the Indian Ocean and miles and miles of white sand. None of the villagers ventured to the sea because of dangerous spirits which perhaps had some basis in the existence of sharks basking in the warm water.

After two weeks there, it was back to the cities – Mombasa and Kampala where we again became housed with local families. In my case this was an African family who lived in Entebbe, the centre of administration on the shores of Lake Victoria. My host was a geologist who had spent much time with the Karamajong in Northern Uganda prospecting for water sources. I learnt from Kamilla his wife how to cook with an absolute minimum of equipment– a sharp knife and a pounder being all that was required. Their children were boarding with their cousins where there was a good school and in the holidays all the children would stay with them. This sharing of children was a non-possessive and practical arrangement that seemed to work well.

I did get to Makere University where I met one of the Sussex students who was temporarily teaching there. We also went on days out including a visit to the kingdom of Toro where there is a photo of us all with the King who only a year later lost his position when Obote took over the whole country. Sadly when Amin went and the kingdoms were restored in 1997 the King of Toro only lived for a year and died young. We also visited Ruanda and the mountains of the moon where we met pigmies who gave me a homemade knife in exchange for my pink sunhat.

And so the six weeks came to an end – not quite. On our way home the plane crash-landed at Luxor, which led to an extra night being put up care of the airline and a trip round the temples. The plane limped on to Rome where there was further engine trouble leading to a change of plane. Two days after setting off we arrived at Heathrow,(or was it Gatwick?). Apparently the destination kept changing leaving my boyfriend in a constant spin. I was somewhat disorientated at Heathrow airport

– on one side of immigration there were fond farewells – would I ever see these comrades again? – on the other was a set of steps down to the arrivals hall where Mark and my settled existence back in UK awaited.

I kept up with the Indian family who were expelled two years later along with all the Uganda Asians. They settled in Canada. I kept up with one of the Asian workcamp volunteers from Mombasa who I later saw in the UK where I learnt the ante-natal building remained much as we had left it half built and unused. I also met the American in our group who the following summer passed through Heathrow en route for another African adventure. Over time, however, these contacts were lost.

4

Back to the Real World

After graduating, Mark got a good job in a national chemical firm in Manchester. I stretched my wings in the depths of multi-racial Peckham - a boys' comprehensive Catholic school where I was the first woman teacher on supply. Mark very quickly worked out that the world of industry was not for him. No matter we were both earning well and most weekends we met up either in London or Manchester. But the rows on Sunday evening caused us to think again about a commuting relationship and the last straw was a Polish Catholic landlady who flung open the door in the middle of the night and threw us out. We arranged to get married. This was to all intents and purposes a pragmatic arrangement. My father asked if I wanted a wedding or money and I said the latter. There was a register office in Tunbridge Wells followed by a family dinner a night at the Cricketers in Brighton and a party for our friends in the London flat.

I easily found a post in a Manchester school up the Oldham Road I took over a class from a man who reputedly resorted at regular intervals to a bottle of whisky in the class cupboard. The desks were in serried ranks and pencils had to be counted out and counted in at the start and end of each lesson. I taught English and relied on avant guard books which had been written to guide the teacher in methods to rein in disaffected students. The culture shock of mini-skirted Sussex University in the 60's and a mill school barely out of the Victorian age could not have been greater.

I dutifully cyclostyled poems such as 'The End of the World' and every now and then managed a glimmer of cooperation. The early morning bus journey across Manchester from Whalley Range through flattened Hume where every now and then a block of preconstructed cabins rose up in towers behind the university area was dreary in the extreme. In the staff room the men sat in a row on one side and the women on the other. I saw no kindred spirit. Then it was wet dinner hour and my turn came to be on duty. This meant, as I understood it, that the entire school had to be packed into two classrooms opposite each other with a corridor inbetween. Probably one was for girls and the other boys. There were children everywhere, perched on every possible sill and surface. Following instructions I put all my weight against the door to prevent children spilling out. Dinner hour over, I marched along angrily to the aged headmaster's office and inquired if I had understood aright because if I did it seemed a most crazy arrangement. He replied in kind and I walked away from his room and from the school for evermore.

We had an attic flat in a new landlady's house. She was kind to us but the winter was not and we often awoke to find the blankets wet with condensation. We longed for something warmer and different and with my Nigerian experience in mind we began to send letters in many directions to African countries. For some reason we were turned down by VSO. Eventually we got a positive response from a teacher training college run by the Catholic mission in Bo, an up-country town in Sierra Leone. We wanted a year's contract. Father 0'Reilly was willing to accept us knowing in advance that we would be breaking a two year contract. We also found that one of Mark's friends who was doing a teacher training course in Bath lived in a most idyllic farmhouse and we stayed there from time to time. So we escaped. But our first year 'in the world' was not an easy one.

Sierra Leone

If I was hoping for a repeat of my Nigerian experience I could only be disappointed. 1968 was well before the civil war (so well described in 'The Memory of Love' by Aminatta Forna.) The teacher training college was not so much an Institute of higher Education as a secondary modern school. There were two streams – one was of mature men who had been teaching for some time and were coming back to complete their education, the other was of secondary school boys. Once more I was in an all-male Catholic environment. Catholicism was not a problem. The Irish fathers were delightfully irreverent, humane men who had a sense of mission and purpose. Brother Gabriel lived with them: an elderly man who had spent most of his life there, he had no thought of returning to a country which he would no longer have known. He was continually being rescued from various parts of the town where he ended up rather the worse for drink. He dispensed sweets to the children and was a popular figure. Probably being a woman was not such a problem for the students as women were not known for their subservience in the local societies.

My job was to teach history- Sierra Leonean history- as well as English. This meant I learned a fair bit about the country which had been used in the nineteenth century along the coastal area as a new society to repatraite slaves from America Freetown was the centre of Creole society and the Creoles considered themselves to be well educated and quite separate from the local tribes of which two were dominant. We lived in the Mende area. The colonial government had, with indirect rule, managed to keep tensions at bay but with independence the crucial competition for power began and was part of the background to the desperate wars decades later.

We joined the local club where we were joined by several local Kenyan volunteers It was a not very splendid remnant of the colonial era to which the dozen or so white teachers belonged and some members of the business community among them two or three Lebanese families. Basically it was a hut with a bar and a rundown tennis court outside. After the teaching day which ended somewhere around two, we had a soup based lunch followed by a siesta leaving a second start to the day around 5.00pm – just time for tennis and a drink before supper cooked by Kaili. Against our principles we had hired Kaili. It was made clear to us that this was expected and was providing work and an income for a local person who would otherwise be without. It was also pointed out that in the tropical climate it would be too stressful to attempt full time work and household chores which all had to be done by hand.

We lived in a house owned by a Lebanese woman who had a shop to one side of the house. She was very proud of the pomegranate tree in the yard. The fathers had rented it for us as the houses on the campus of the teacher training college were already allocated.

Towards the end of our year, a spate of violent robberies was conducted against the white community. Men wielding machetes forced an entrance and injured the inhabitants inside. This always seemed to happen between 1.00am and 5.00am and made for an uncertain sleep pattern. Our turn came very close to the end of our stay. Although we had a night watchman, and perhaps even because we had a night watchman, we awoke to hear the back door being attacked. We ran out of the front onto the main road. Soon we were being pursued and Mark with some presence of mind stopped to bribe the youths in order to give me time to get away. We had little enough to steal or to lose except our bodies. It was a nasty shock that's all. Yet it overshadows much of my memory. There are no great memories of beautiful crafts or a happy people. I do not recall that we made any African friends there and were relieved to return to UK.

We did, however, team up with some American teachers to go on a trek north. There was one delightful encounter with a village that may never before have seen Europeans. It was a village with round mud huts such as you see in all the picture books. The children especially the boys wore their long hair in coiled plats. There was a river with a bathing area for men and a separate area for the women. As we gathered in the assembly hut everyone came to peer at us. Although we didn't use the creeper bridges, we saw several on our trek which lasted the best part of a week. We perhaps got an idealised glimpse of a way of life which had not been overtaken by modernisation . However, the sense of community, order and sustainability chimes with many a green sense of returning to a more meaningful Arcadia.

5

Comfort zone: Found and Lost

We returned to Sussex with a difference. Not only were we married but we lived in Lewes for the first time. We took over a rented house from close friends who went on to pursue academia in Wales. Mark had a place to do a Ph.D and I wanted to firm up my teaching experience by getting a teaching qualification. We were Sussex university students once more.

My training involved being a part-time teacher in a small rural secondary modern school with a teaching partner and a teacher mentor. I really enjoyed making an archive kit as part of my teaching project. Mark was involved with computers in an era when one computer occupied a small room and information had to be punched in. It was a very nurturing year.

I continued to teach on supply both back at the school where I had done my teaching practice and in and around Brighton. The main event of the post training year however, was becoming a mother. This followed an anxious wait as the pill delayed my ability to get pregnant. Even so I was unprepared for the changes that happened around me. I had a number of friends and acquaintances, some who had stayed on from undergraduate days, and some I met as fellow mothers-to-be. My daughter was born two weeks premature.. The hospital incorrectly gauged that Mark had time to go home for supper. My daughter was born a few minutes after his return. She soon showed signs of jaundice. The old-fashioned maternity unit was run by an ex-army captain and feeding involved mathematical measurements and weighings such that I was unable to relax enough to breast feed and unable to leave. It was a very long 10 days before we were allowed home and Mark at once took to a relaxed bottle feeding schedule.

His research work allowed some flexibility. I think he stayed home two days! As he set off leaving me in front of the coal fire and holding the baby I experienced a deep sense of abandonment and there were no close relatives or friends who I could ask to stay to tide me over.

Life got better when we moved into our own much larger house. The town council had granted us a mortgage on the basis of three times our student grants. We figured out that by letting out two rooms at £2 a week each we could completely cover the mortgage cost.

An old lady had died in the house leaving what the estate agent dismissed as a load of junk. I still have a lovely old wooden and glass bookcase from there and overall the 'junk' turned out to be worth almost a quarter of the price we paid for the house. Within a year we had done the house up – that is to say we had had a kitchen made in the basement, night storage heaters installed, and the wiring fixed. Our DIY skills were limited to decorating in purple and orange – 70's colours. The hall was bottle green.

Looking back it seems astonishing that within a year what we had achieved fell so badly apart. We had the marriage, the baby who slept through much of the night, the house and good economic prospects. We were just 27 and 28. But when I turned down a full time job offer at a good girls' grammar school I knew that I was not ready to settle down and moreover that I was not going to continue in teaching. I was offered a place on a Master's course in Race Relations at Bristol University. We discussed the practicalities of my doing this and Mark was encouraging. I don't remember at that stage – perhaps it was the March before the course began – whether we all intended to make a temporary base in

Bristol or whether I was going to commute on a weekly basis. I accepted the place and so began a summer of branching out.

We belonged to a baby sitting group of couples attached to the university in some form or another. It gradually emerged that some of the original members were having extra-marital relationships within the group. At the same time there was news of a new Women's Movement. We women formed a group based mainly but not exclusively on the babysitting circle. One thing led to another and it seemed Mark was in great demand. As always up for a new experience I encouraged the idea that we might have other sexual relationships. But neither of us was prepared for the emotional fallout and my efforts to halt things must have seemed burdensomely controlling. Out of these experiments came the notion of creating a commune. I was by that time a nervous wreck and thankfully escaped to Bristol whilst the babysitting cum women's group rented a house together. I do not remember the details of the collapse of this arrangement. I was always persona non grata there. It's possible the kids had a good year.

Bristol opened my eyes. The Women's' Movement was very big there, second only to London. There were Women's conferences, Women's music, Feminist cabaret which I took part in, alternative relationships, building a world without men

'a woman without a man is like a fish without a bicycle'.

There was a euphoric feeling of power, of a world about to change.

I had already encountered alternatives to the family – first in Nigeria where there were a number of single parent and polygamous families, then in Israel where women were almost entirely free from child care responsibilities as the children were brought up on the Kibbutz collectively. I did not feel that I had sole responsibility for my daughter and quite accepted that her father could be the main parent or, that she could be part of a collective responsibility in Lewes. In the second term at Bristol, I moved into a shared flat with a sort of pantry next to my basement room and had my daughter stay. She spent the morning with a childminder closeby, the afternoon with me and I worked in my room in the evening once she had gone to bed. During this time I had a visit from an outraged landlady who arranged for a social worker to check out that she was not being neglected.

In the last term, however, Naomi returned to Lewes and I had more time for my dissertation. This was an exposé of the decisions and documentation that led to the closure of the inner city school in the 'black' areas resulting in black children being dispersed to large outer city comprehensive schools. I called it Bussing in Bristol. The professor complete with bow tie was not at all encouraging. Possibly with delicate funding in mind he wanted aspects of race relations in the nineteenth century to be researched – much safer. I felt I had potentially quite a coup as the county was in the process of being reorganised and the documents I was looking at were due to be destroyed. I say potentially a coup because I never published the dissertation or made an article out of it. Fortunately I had the support of another member of staff - the youngest and in many ways the most vulnerable – so I appreciated his go ahead. A third member of staff asked if I would prefer to become a social worker in St Paul's. The implication being that I should leave. Notwithstanding I got my Masters.

That summer, I met an American woman at a feminist conference who was looking for someone to take up a research post in Women's Studies at the Science Studies Unit in Edinburgh where her husband worked. There was some urgency as the funding had to be immediately allocated or lost. Things happened within a week. I was interviewed, met a research student who invited me back to his commune for tea, was offered a place there with my daughter, and bingo I was on my own path once more. I write of this glibly. It was a traumatic time. In retrospect, I was very attached to Mark and held on to the idea for several years that we would get back and live together with our daughter. I only finally let go when Mark wrote in some wrath that he needed my permission to be sterilised: his current partner (a member of the ex-women's group) was uncomfortable with other forms of contraception. We formally divorced some years later in 1979.

6

Communes

When I joined the Edinburgh 'Commune' it had become more of a Community with income contributed on a sliding scale rather than all-out financial sharing. Started by a group of university students who were members of the Student Christian movement in the early 70's the predominant ideology had changed to International Socialism by the time I first went to tea. I watched this on the sidelines. The majority of members were very committed to the cause and there was quite a militant command structure – for example cars could be commandeered at a moment's notice for a demonstration. There was much zeal distributing the Socialist Worker.

The house was a large semi-detached built by an Admiral some hundred years earlier. There were some imposing features such as a large wooden mantelpiece in the sitting room and several of the rooms were very generous in size. Even in August it was necessary to have some form of heat and we depended on fitted gas fires or in my case a portable electric fire. When at one point it was suggested that we progress to central heating there was a protest. This would have been partly a matter of finance but it was also an objection to bourgeois values.

I stayed there for several years whilst I made some headway with my Ph.D. Two of us were living on grants like myself, the poorer members were on the dole and one or two had professional salaries. There was little conflict about money, mainly because there was enough to go round and we were substantially responsible for our own extras. There was a communal meal every evening cooked by two members on a rota. No washing up machine. The men tended to cook from recipe books and the women from experience. The male cooks were often more successful! There was a strong egalitarian ethic. Various people offered to share in childcare – taking my daughter to school and so on and I had sharing arrangements with people outside. One of the advantages of moving into an existing community of 10 members was that I was immediately put in contact with friends of friends and a much larger community. Thus I met like-minded mums who were happy to liaise over childcare. If I wanted to go out of an evening there were almost always people who were in and available to check on her. It worked very well for me as a single mother and she got a lot of attention. She stayed in Edinburgh in the term time and with her father in Lewes in the holidays.

There was a major structural change when the people who had originally obtained a mortgage to buy the property wanted to leave and get their own mortgage. We created a new structure with the aid of a Housing Association and the Housing Corporation such that any current member was a member of the association but lost it on leaving. I was nominally the Chairman. The proviso was that if at any time all the members left, the house would revert to the Housing Corporation. As far as I know this was a one-off structure and ensured the longevity of the project. It was certainly in existence some fifteen years ago because my daughter visited it.

In 1974 the Edinburgh Women's movement did not as yet have the momentum of the Bristol women but it was not long before I was part of a new women's group to which some of the commune women came. We were concerned with the politics of health, the sort of relationships that were possible, our sexuality, who we were apart from our conditioning, our common experiences as women and most importantly to support each other in our day to day hassles. It was a very different sharing from the gropings of the first women's group in Lewes. We were concerned with the patriarchal society, the laws that discriminated against us, and to a lesser extent the position of third world women. Nationally there was a burgeoning of literature and campaigns. I belonged to a national feminist history group in which others such as Sheila Rowbotham eventually became known and published. It was what my life including my thesis was about for a long period of time. The impact of it has been lifelong. Somehow it made sense of my mother's and my grandmother's forms of depression and oppression. It was a Eureka moment to realise that the world was made by and for men and that here was a rare opportunity to change all that. I became very angry for at least two years. Much was indeed achieved, both personally and world wide. But it was of course only a start. By the mid 80's it seems the steam had gone out of the movement as a whole and it is only now (2012) and in a smaller way that young women are speaking out again.

Relationships were a little more fluid in the community than in straight society and there were attempts to be non- possessive but there were some very sticky times and it was hard work being alternative and anti -

family. In the community the International Socialist paradigm had given way to a feminist one and previously heterosexual women had relationships with each other. Couples broke up or left if they found the going too hard. I had to seek respite for a time back in Bristol but soon returned to find considerable support.

Meanwhile one woman, a teacher, went off to India and came back in orange. I was fascinated by her tales of transformation, of the Indian mystic who was called Bhagwan. On the one hand it seemed so much hocus pocus and on the other there seemed to be something in it. I began to read his books. They were not writings but discourses that had been written down. What he said had a ring of truth. But it was not a political movement, quite the reverse. It was a key, an opening to go beyond words, politics, and worldly dilemmas. Certainly it was worth a look.

Meanwhile, my time in Edinburgh came to an end as did my part ownership of a house in Bristol.(It was not a house that I ever lived in but it preserved my financial share of the ex-marital home.) With the proceeds I bought a flat in downtown Montpelier one road away from St Paul's in Bristol before it became chic. My flat was a modernised maisonette with a flat roof which had fantastic views. It had been created out of an old terraced house. The downstairs maisonette was owned by a couple of rather particular librarians who were at times distraught at the goings on upstairs. (At the time I was into cathartic therapy). The house looked on to an empty space which used to house two or three terraced houses and had perhaps been bombed or at least demolished leaving odd walls and reminders of what had been. Next to this was a pub. Down the road was Herbert's bakery. It soon sported a cafe where the treat was breakfast with croissant and apricot jam. In a nearby crammed street was an early incarnation of a wholefood veggie shop, a little further on a traditional Italian grocery. It was a place encouraging enterprise with at one time a wholesome café and also a pottery which for a short time I had a third share of whilst the potter herself went away to India. It straddled the old and the new. There was a drunk who lived on the street, and who harmlessly fell down stairways into basements. There was the bird man (who walked up and down with bird food). On Sundays a man walked through shouting his wares – the Sunday papers which he pulled in a cart behind him. Beyond was an apostolic church which gave voice loudly on a Sunday morning. I felt at home on these margins. Presumably all this characters are now long gone and the houses gentrified almost beyond recognition. It was here that I completed my Ph.D thesis financed by an early morning cleaning job at the Health centre round the corner and rent from the spare room in my flat.

7

Poona 1979

It was six years before the thesis was finished. I was at a Feminist History Conference that summer when a sense of exhaustion overcame me. In the Autumn, I handed in my bound thesis and took off for the Commune of Bhagwan Shree Rajneesh in India. I had three months for this experience after arranging to be back in time for Christmas with my daughter.

I was so keen to see the mystic in person that the first early morning after my arrival found me sitting in his lecture space outside his house with a heightened sense of anticipation which swept me through the rigid protocol which surrounded his appearances. Bags had to be left in a safe area. I had no local currency as yet but strangers paid for me. The entrance was met by sniffers who ensured that no odour of any kind particularly perfume was to be found as Bhaghwan was sensitive and allergic. Marshals organised the crosslegged bodies sitting in silence on the marble floor and any sign of a cough meant immediate eviction. There was a pregnant wait.

He floated in in a way that suggested he was beyond a sense of time, a sense of mind. His namaste was prolonged and his gaze seemed to take in everyone there (some several hundred of us). He spoke in Hindi for an hour and left as seamlessly as he entered.

My carefully dyed orange clothes were out of date. The predominant colour was now maroon. Changing colour was the least of my problems in adjusting. The only accommodation in the Ashram was for long term residents, people who were in charge of the running of the Ashram and Bhagwan's mother who had a small apartment. Everyone else contributed to the local economy by living outside. I had a friend who had arranged for me to have the other mattress in her room for a week whilst I settled in. Rats rattled around the roof. There was a communal washing space at the end of the veranda. Monkeys chattered in the trees outside and the nets could barely keep out the mosquitoes.It was all extremely basic. Within two days I had acquired both kinds of dysentery. No sooner had I got over that than I had jardias – another intestinal parasite- something one just lived with until getting back home. My living situation was extremely fluid – I notched up some 16 different locations. Finally I ended up sharing a hut in a sannyasin encampment by the river some 15 mins walk away. It was idyllic and there was a sense of community within the huts which had been assembled out of straw panels sewn together. In the evening after discourse we walked back together in the dark for safety and someone would light a fire and play a guitar.

But the Ashram was really where I lived. There were showers and toilets and places to eat. From 7.00am until 11.00pm there was a programme of meditations and allied activities. Generally people participated in the plethora of therapy groups 'to spring clean the mind' for meditation at the same time as doing the largely active meditations Bhagwan had devised over a number of years as being appropriate for his western followers. Dynamic at 7.00am is the most vigorous. It involves altering breathing patterns with a cathartic element so that the day can begin fresh from the past. Most days at 8.00am Bhagwan gave a discourse and a programme continued through the day. Many nationalities were there especially the Germans and the Japanese. Aside from listening to the content of Bhagwan's discourses – and he was extraordinarily erudite – one caught his presence. In fact there became something almost dreamlike about being among his sannyasins. It was a feeling of tremendous peace and acceptance of whatever was thrown at you. It was quite difficult to negotiate something outside the Ashram like getting a bank transfer or sending a telegram without spacing out. It was not that everything went smoothly. Rather the place was designed to continually upset expectations it seemed. In some ways one fell apart and there was a sense of being without a safety net. The more experienced sannyasins were given Work. This was seen as a privilege and was regarded as a 'Group' in itself. A gardener for example might be set to construct a walled bed one day and be told to take it down the next ie a lesson of not getting attached to one's creation. The purpose of work was not so much getting things done though a lot did have to be done but to learn to be meditative in action. The Germans were very good at giving orders and all sorts of protocol had to be obeyed around the toilets, for example, not to mention the system of getting into the lecture space mentioned before. Renowned academics would be assigned to the lowliest of duties in the process of losing their ego.

After I had been there a week, and with some ambivalence I asked to become a sannyasin and so the evening came when I sat a few feet away from Bhagwan while he gave me my mala, my name and sannyas. He said that if I stuck around my life would be transformed and although the ambivalence remained I reckon my life did over the next 21 years become transformed. In what ways? Hard to pin down. There is a certain detachment a certain acceptance, letting things happen. I rarely feel involved enough to be angry. I do not have much of a sense of urgency and I can easily tap into an inner sense of calm. I have no fear of death and in general am where I want to be in life. I am certainly not enlightened but I am lighter and far away from that desperate feeling that life is too much of a burden to be lived and the imperative to struggle against all the injustices of the world.

8

What next?

I returned from Poona and completed the transition to living as a sannyasin. I threw out all my non-red clothes. I attended a viva for my Ph.D once the problem of finding examiners was solved. It was a study in ideas about female sexuality leading to the ideas made famous by Marie Stopes in 'Married Love'. The examiners were not impressed. They wanted to give me an M.Phil or have me re-write it with a chronological structure. There was no guarantee that the (new) set of examiners would not prefer the structure as it was (sets of ideas). I had few regrets about walking away and no interest in engaging further with the politics of academia. A kind person later said that it was 'before my time'.

At the age of 35, I still had no career direction and set about applying for a variety of jobs which did not require a particular training. In the end I became part of a Night Shelter team in Hammersmith but only for six months. We were an idealistic team of which I was the oldest member and my conscientiousness irritated those who had in some ways more experience, that is to say they had been night shelter clients. They had walked the streets, slept in the bins, done the round of homeless shelters, driven by alcoholism or dysfunction of some sort.

The staff lived on the first floor of the building and the ground floor opened every evening to the clients. We stayed up all night when on shift and I sat with people drying out, with people wanting company or who couldn't sleep.

One night we found a man collapsed in the gent's toilet. We called an ambulance but he was not, they deemed, an appropriate referral. We called social services night team. Unfortunately, and I forget the reason, perhaps because he had no fixed abode, it was not within their remit to assist. Gaps like that existed. The night shelter performed one very useful service. Inmates were given a week's accommodation and though it took many hours visiting the local social security office, since they now had a fixed address, they could claim social security. I remember mostly men. There were young runaways, and older men: one always presented an immaculate appearance and carried a small suitcase: casualties of the system and the family; the bottom of the pile.

I returned to my flat in Bristol. At about this time Bhagwan moved to the United States where his disciples had purchased an unused 100 square mile ranch in Oregon: the Ashram in Poona effectively closed (a skeleton staff of local inhabitants looked after it). This meant there were many sannyasins wandering about from one place to another until the Oregon site was ready to take on workers. A few came to Bristol and I offered one of them a room in my flat. One thing led to another, we became lovers and together we set up a meditation centre. This was a new experience for us – we had to find and rent premises. We found a building that had been some sort of factory close to the centre of Bristol in a Victorian complex of disused buildings. Another group had taken on the ground floor, where they had set up a vegetarian café. Doing up the first floor was a total renovation job financed by donations. The work itself was unpaid and I had the experience of managing volunteers with all sorts of trips about being told or asked to do something. Because the sannyasin community has a broad following most skills and work experience were, and are, available in one form or another.

Within a month or so we had a large floor space – the whole area of the building with a small office and toilet off– available for the centre programme. As well as twice daily meditations, we invited some of the group leaders from Poona to lead therapy groups – usually over a weekend. These were popular since the group leaders who had been in Poona had been rarely available in Europe. The team running the centre got to lead meditations perhaps for the first time and so it was a learning curve for all of us. I myself learnt the joys and tribulations of being a manager with a volunteer work force. It was a relatively short lived experience because the hub of the sannyasin organisation in England based in a mansion in Suffolk wanted us to look for a more salubrious venue and when one materialised on Brandon Hill the whole process began again with a different team. There was a great sense that with clear objectives anything could happen though some might say Bhagwan made it happen. When the ranch at Oregon took off, a dedicated work force was needed and with the same single mindedness (or meditative awareness) a city complete with a huge dam rose out of the muddy buffalo ranch. There were annual festivals to which thousands came. I visited but did not have the exhilarating experience of being part of its exponential growth. Those who could and did often spoke of it as the highlight of their life.

So the quest(ion) continued … what next?

9

A career at last?

Although I had spent much of my adult life in education both as a teacher and as a student, I lacked any formal training apart from 9 months as a teacher – a career I had put aside at least as far as teaching in secondary education in the UK. With my brief experience of the night shelter on my CV I was able to get a place on the graduate social work training in Bristol. In particular I was interested in becoming a medical social worker. My placement at Bristol Royal Infirmary (BRI) was dramatic and enriching, especially as I had a mentor who was innovative and confident and taught me much not least how to manage her own disability (she had had polio and was could only get about my means of a wheelchair).

Several clients stay in my mind. I was called to a cardiac ward to see an eighty year old woman who had been raped. When emergencies were admitted to the hospital they had to be placed, at least initially, in whichever ward there was a space. The problem was although the bed was free it was in the cardiology ward and much needed for cardiac patients. The woman it turned out had been a recluse for some 20 years. A man wearing a balaclava had broken into her terraced house and abused her. She was in an awful state of shock. It was a front page story on the evening paper. In my role of social worker (student) I got to know her, and had to advise the medical team whether her home situation was tenable so that she could be discharged. It was clear that she needed to be kept in a safe place (ie the hospital) until she had come to terms with the worst aspect of the trauma: it was also unclear whether it would ever be tenable to return to her home and that alternative accommodation would have to be found. These things inevitably took time. A junior doctor was livid at the delay and wrote his anger into the patient's notes. Enter my supervisor who wheeled herself into the situation and forcefully put the social and psychological needs of the patient firmly in their place.

There was another case of a man who was dying. The medical staff had informed the social work department that the consultant was due to tell him 'the news' that day and that it might be helpful if someone went to see him. My supervisor suggested that I meet up with him in advance of receiving 'the news' before going a second time afterwards. At the first visit, he was bright and looking forward to the things he was going to do when he got out. It was not my job to disabuse him. When I saw him a second time several hours later he had given up completely. All hope had been taken away, he had let go and died a few days later.

At that time I had not had much contact with death. The Bristol Hospice put on a course on Dying in which we wrote our own obituaries. A positive take on a cancer death was proposed – in the first place that pain control was very advanced and effective such that one could remain conscious to the end and secondly one had notice of the time scale and so could put one's affairs in order and say one's goodbyes.

I learnt to be around terminally ill people and my work generally consisted of creating a sort of anonymous safe space where the dying person could talk about how it was for them away from their relations whose job it was to maintain a cheerful environment.

After the course I immediately got a short locum post in a geriatric hospital and that was followed by a locum maternity leave post in Clifton District. By this time I had a good reference and a chance of forging a career I thought. But when I became pregnant I made little headway at job interviews. I hoped to be able to return some day.

10

My son

The day I learned I was pregnant we had just moved from my central Bristol flat in Montpelier to a terraced house in the country some 13 miles away. The plan had been that I would get a permanent social work job for a year or two and *then* have another child. Instead I was in the middle of nowhere it seemed with partner making the commute into Bristol and nearest friend some 5 miles away. I felt in an uncanny way I was reliving my mother's life .She and my father had left London for a rural backwater in Buckinghamshire when I was a year old. We both seemed fated to seek a rural idyll and become very isolated and depressed. For starters I could not have a home birth because I was too far from the nearest hospital if anything went wrong. There was a slight improvement on the birth of my daughter in that I got out of hospital two hours after the birth and was transferred for one night to the local hospital. However, barely a week later we were back in hospital again, this time in the paediatric ward because my son had developed a sore on his skin which threatened to be a rare disease. It wasn't. But I was very upset when he was given antibiotics at such an early age. I had also demanded that his father stay home for the first two weeks which was an essential help as I found with breastfeeding there was little else I could do. He was a large baby and drank a lot! It was a case of sitting with a pot of tea, holding the baby all day long. Fortunately he slept well at night right from the beginning. However, it was decided that I was not producing enough milk (at six weeks) and he did seem to take to the bottle with gusto. It was a lonely time punctuated by visits to and from friends with similar aged babies and some visits to a small club pool which was warmer than the local baths.

Some months later I was very relieved to be offered the opportunity to put on an adult education course with one of the staff of the local college of further education. It was a course for Women Returner's and we called it 'Second Step'. Initially it took place for two hours a week but it soon expanded and eventually developed follow up add-ons. Of course I too was finding out what opportunities there were for women who had children and wanted to get back into the work force. It was also my first introduction (and theirs) to computers. In fact the following year I was offered a newly conceived half time post as 'Wider Opportunities Worker'. Meanwhile I was meeting up with interesting women in adult education and in women's management courses. But then the college faced bankruptcy and my post was the first one to go.

On the gloomy side it can be seen that all my attempts at career making were doomed to become cul-de-sacs. But shortlived as these initiatives were, I think they had a value: they touched other's lives in an intangible way and although dispiriting it led in my own life to varied experiences. The dispiriting thing was not so much a door closing that had promised to stay open but the haphazard injustices that often went with it. In the case of the college job for example, there were two Wider Opportunities workers and only one could be kept on. It was explained that the other person needed the post more than me!

Before gaining the not-so-permanent job, however, and before my son's father left, there was another adventure. We went to explore the possibility of living abroad in Greece. The story lies not so much in the two months we spent on the islands of Lesbos and Skyros (January and February 1987) as in the journey to get there – referred to by my son as the journey to Snowmanland.

The cheapest way to get to Greece, my travel agent informed me was to take Romanian airlines. It involved a short transfer in Bucharest for onward travel to Athens. My partner had organised a two month unpaid leave from work and we had let out our terraced cottage so all was set for an exploratory trip.

I had been to Greece before and it had seemed an idyllic place fulfilling all the stereotypes yet with an opportunity to pursue one's own adventures. It was a culture where there were blankets of reassurance as in, 'No problem', 'No problem' – music to the ears of a perpetually anxious person like myself. Might it be a good place to bring up a child? A few days after Xmas we left. I remember standing at the busstop in 4 degrees (Fahrenheit) full of anticipation.

We entered the plane to funereal music– sombre chords – in economical surroundings or so it seemed before the era of low cost airlines. Our fellow passengers were bound for a range of destinations including two cyclists; minimally clad; heading for a cycling holiday in Egypt.

As we approached Romania there was an announcement that weather conditions precluded landing in Bucharest: we were instead landing at Timisuara just on the border. We were duly escorted to a hotel and would proceed to Bucharest in all probability the next day. The evening meal was somewhat surreal due to lack of heating in subzero temperatures: the waiters wore Russian style fur hats and we wore everything we could lay our hands on given that we had no access to our hold luggage. There was rice I remember and rather little of anything else. Still the next day we were on our way to the capital and once again a grand but essentially ill-equipped hotel. Our onward connection to Athens had long since left and there would be a several days before the next flight. Yes we could have places on it.

One developed strategies. Our room was several floors up and perfectly adequate. On looking out one saw a large portrait of Ceausescu, hanging down a building some 14 storeys high Since there was minimal and possibly no heating, we invited all and sundry into our room and exploited the body heat. In return we had a small travel jug with which we could brew tea. Next problem was lack of nappies.

We were directed to a large department store some few blocks from the hotel in search of nappies. The department store was virtually empty of goods but full of people who formed a fast moving trail up and down and through the store in case by chance there was something of value to them. No nappies obviously. I settled on tea towels instead.

We wrapped up and tried to go out for a walk or two. Snow formed a thick wall between us and the road. My partner venturing further found himself at gunpoint outside Ceausescu's palace. He beat a hasty retreat. The departure airport was similarly guarded. I went out for a breath of fresh air and had to negotiate a gun to get back in. Our bags were searched by a large sinister looking woman in a dark place where one could imagine disappearing without trace.

Having a small child to take care of was a thread of normality which I clung to in this frightening third world European place of enormously wide streets where splendidly dressed armies must have paraded. A human touch was a piece of cake given to us by the cleaner. Imagining how little she must have, I was reluctant to deprive her of it.

A few days later found us sitting in a Greek café outside eating the most enormous and voluptuous breakfast. I could not somehow believe that we had got back on track and that that parallel world of deprivation and cold existed.

We went first of all to the island of Lesbos which was within sight of Turkey. I had read of a women's collective which let out rooms to tourists. This was, however, in the summer. Nevertheless we did not have long to wait on the quay side before we were taken to a woman who let out rooms. Actually it was a self-contained unit, ideally tiled for the summer heat but cold and damp in the winter. We stayed there a month and then made for Skyros where I had had a holiday some years earlier.

In February there was a festival on Skyros that takes place over three weekends based on the dance of the goatman. I forget the story. It involved a goatherd losing his flock and taking on the skin of a goat and dancing. There were processions of goatmen and the taverns and streets all filled up with visitors and Athenians who were coming back to their roots. Having mingled with the crowd we retired to our back street room and looked out from the balcony to see a middle aged man dancing alone and almost possessed up the deserted street. The graceful movement against the backcloth of the starry night was quite magical.

We returned to our house in England a little earlier than planned and were immediately swallowed up by the day to day need to earn a living with no particular time to think about the future. Sadly we realised that it was not to be a joint future and so I became a single parent.

11

Single parent again

From the time I knew I was pregnant I worried about schools. The terrace we had moved to was part of an ex-coal mining area and was deeply traditional. This was reflected in the local primary schools where I would not have survived the playground for a moment. Hence when my son was 3, I moved back to Bristol and sought out the Steiner school which was a humane, intimate sort of place. It demanded a lot of parental commitment both in terms of keeping costs down but also on a psychological level where the parents became part of the community. I appreciated this but it made it very difficult to contemplate working when children had to be picked up every morning and sponge cakes made for a cake sale every week. However, what came my way was a free women's six month woodwork course with paid childcare. I had always wanted to make things and I loved the smell and look of wood.

It was the high point of being a single parent and I learnt a great deal. 'Cutting

Edge' as the training premises were called was unfortunately soon afterwards closed down when its funding was cut. This was a blow as we had been allowed to continue using the machines in the workshop after the course had finished.

Some of us got on to another free course in Dorset at Hooke Parke. The purpose of this project was to create uses for small round wood timber and so reduce the amount of imported timber. Some innovative structures had been made out of small timbers in tension. For me it was a wonderful six week holiday in the woods making bridges and structures, learning about the structures of different woods, and something about forestry all catered and paid for. My son stayed with his father.

Just before I set off for India again, his father decided that he could not after all have our son to stay. I had saved enough money for six months which was the longest stretch of time I spent in Poona. There were many adventures there, therapy groups, lovers, health scares and so on. The straw huts had been replaced by concrete blocks of flats, one of which I rented advantageously placed next to the Kid's Commune. I could leave my son for the day and if necessary the night.

The Kids Commune was run by sannyasins and for long afterwards my son remembered some of the children from around the world he met there. He learnt about massage and watched performances from the man with Charlie the monkey, the magician, and the man with a cobra in a basket. He climbed up the creeper on the trees. He also had to take part in the chores such as sweeping up after tea. The kids were brought into the main Commune at lunch time to be with their parents. It was reminiscent of the Kibbutz experience and was in some ways hard for both of us. All in all I was glad when his father who had missed him agreed to look after him for the remaining months I was away. We went to Mumbai by train and spent the afternoon on Juhu beach where there was a camel ride. The owner of a cloth shop opposite where we were staying invited us up to meet his family and see his parrot. At the airport we met up with the 14 year son of a friend of mine and the two boys travelled back under the care of the cabin crew. Apparently my son stayed awake the whole journey.

After seeing him off I saw two dazed Japanese sannyasins who had just arrived and were heading for Poona where they needed accommodation. I invited them to share my flat.

12

Devon 1990-2005

The move from Bristol to Devon was partly to do with a feeling of having finished with Bristol over the six months in India, but more to do with being in love with a cellist who was unlike any of the other men I had been with in that he was moody and passionate and so 'in the flow' as to be completely unpredictable. Cellist was in the process of moving from London to Devon. We started life together in a caravan concealed in a farmer's barn on a farm just outside Totnes. We both found odd jobs. Mine as a cleaner on the Dartington estate led in the autumn to a large and beautiful flat. The flat had been a houseparent's flat when Foxhole on the estate was a school set up in the 20's as a progressive boarding school where the pupils had a lot of scope to develop in their own way. Since 1988 when the school closed down the buildings had fallen into some disrepair and were very underused. My flat was in the middle of a wing and looked out over fields towards the main house.

For half of the following six years my cellist partner lived separately and there were many ons and offs in the relationship followed by several years when we had to leave the Dartington estate (1993) and remove to a house the Trust owned in Totnes itself. It was seldom easy following our own paths and looking after a child. This made the times we were in harmony, all the more dramatic and fulfilling. Life continued with a move or two here and there as necessity dictated and with survival in unskilled employment. Apart from part time cleaning and caretaking at Foxhole, I rented a place for two days a week in a wood workshop with a very supportive owner, so that I could keep alive my woodwork skills. I also had a place at the Natural Health centre to practise counselling.

Gradually, however, life settled down and I returned to social work again on a short term basis. The housing et changed so that I was able to sell my house in Bristol and buy a spacious flat in the centre of Totnes. My son could walk to school and had a close knit group of friends most of whom were 'out of school' and my ex-boyfriend found long term accommodation and a water business which enabled him to carry on his creative musical pursuits.

A very small inheritance from my father which arrived at the death of my stepmother enabled me to start training as a family therapist. This proved to be a satisfying synthesis of the fractured work experiences I had had, because to repeat a truism, the more experienced you are, or in my case the more different experiences you have had, the more you are able to appreciate the predicaments of your clients. The theoretical aspect of the training satisfied my academic leanings, and the practical aspects were informed by my counselling, teaching and social work skills. The different family constellations which presented themselves resonated with some of my own experience. Moreover I was in a regular student group who over three years became a substitute for my lack of family. Whilst I was pursuing this course on 1.5 days a week my 3 day a week locum social work post came to an end and I obtained a post as counsellor in North Devon college for 12 hours a week as a college counsellor. These part–time posts changed until I had a 'portfolio' of work over 16 hours a week which triggered family credit and in this way we were able to subsist. I set up a counselling service for the Visually Impaired at Torbay hospital, I gained substantial support from the Adult education officer and this led to coordinating counselling training in Totnes and doing some teaching on it. I worked in my neighbour's stationery shop; I worked in a pie factory and from time to time as a cleaner.

I had given up the idea of getting a 'proper job' until I unexpectedly succeeded at a job interview in Oxford. It was a year's locum family therapist post in a community team and a children's psychiatric hospital. Then, aged 59, I felt my career had begun. But no! The locum did not lead to a permanent post and several other interviews over the following year proved abortive. Finally when a post I was being interviewed for was frozen at lunchtime on the day of the interview itself because of cuts, I thought enough was enough and I took a leap into underfunded retirement.

Meanwhile I had been preparing to fulfil one of my dreams which was to live in France. My flat had a small mortgage and for a very short time I was earning enough to get a further mortgage. (It was also a time when mortgages were easy to get before the crash). Having obtained a mortgage offer which lasted for a period of six months, I had a small window in which to use the money to buy a house in France. After frantic nightly internetting and some visits to a friend in the eastern Pyrenees I had found a house in the south west of

France. Thus at the same time as my work in Oxford finished, I found myself the owner of a small house within sight of the Pyrenees. It was unfortunate that I was nowhere near my friend in the East as house prices over there had risen dramatically when Barcelona second homers took over. Although I had envisaged using the house as a second home in the short term, my age and my difficulties in getting work meant that I gave up or had to give up any career ambition. I felt the frustration for some years afterwards as I felt I had become quite skilled, loved the team work, and perhaps most important of all seemed to be able to facilitate people having the confidence to change their lives.

From 1997 when cellist and I parted I was a single parent. My son's father had stopped giving me any financial support long before. For a time I had paid the fare for my son to travel to his father for alternate weekends as I felt it was so important for the two of them to continue to have a good relationship. I went to a solicitor for advice about how to claim some support from the father. This was not possible as father was one step ahead and had left employment. The solicitor recommended I stopped funding the travel and fortunately his father did take on the cost of this. There were a number of other single mums with sons much the same age and with a high degree of cooperation we achieved a good life for our boys. In fact it was only with the support of these other mums that I managed to keep part-time jobs going. It was always possible to fix up overnighters, or a couple of hours after-school care. One group of mums raised funds for a skate park and a follow–up group, which I was involved in, organised the erection of a half pipe and pipes for grinding on. My son's group of friends progressed from roller blades (aged 9-10) to BMXing (11-17) and in young adulthood to acrobatic snowboarding. I wonder how my son's early experience (aged about a year) when he climbed up in the kitchen to a hatch and leapt down to the sitting room couch on the other side in front of a startled midwife, was a formative experience.

In my son's teenage years, we went camping in a group to north Cornwall. There was a skate park nearby where we could leave the boys whilst us mums made for a sandy cove. One summer a couple of us with sons went to Poland where we taught English at a summer camp in a huge communist built agricultural college. The boys could join in the activities as well as making friends with the other 'teachers' who were mostly students and only a few years older than them.

One afternoon there was a knock at the door of our room and an elderly man introduced himself. He wanted to have English lessons at 5.00pm every day as this was a time we were free. He had a room elsewhere in the block and we had a delightful time reading a text that he provided and drinking tea and cake. He told us a little of his life and how difficult it was to keep to his studies in the war. He had however, by a strange coincidence become a family therapist and worked in an institution in the nearby town. Of course we asked to be taken there. It had been a barracks pre-communism with stables for the regiment and a parade ground. He showed us around. The programme there seemed very humane – horse riding sessions and so on. He himself was waiting for a heart operation in Scandanavia. We tried to keep up with him by letter (email was only just beginning) and rather feared the worst when we didn't get any response.

Another group using the building was the national team of ballroom dancers. We sometimes went over to watch. They had a punishing day of acrobatic dancing training the like of which I had never seen though now (2011) that 'Strictly' has hit the scene it might not have seemed so impressive.

In return for our teaching, we were treated to 'A Grand Tour of Poland.

Unfortunately our transport turned out to be a satellite van which lacked windows. No matter we got around, had adventures, and realised how well off we were compared with the people we met.

Given my Jewish background, I particularly wanted to visit Auschwitz. I was presented with a sanitised afternoon's jaunt around nicely painted wood and brick structures into which I was invited to see tastefully displayed museum exhibits. There were walls of portraits of mainly Polish people who had crossed the Reich for some reason or another, been sentenced by the Gestapo 'court' usually to be summarily shot, indoors if there were only a couple or outside against a wall which now looked sculptural, laden with flowers and letters. There was a room covered with golden straw to convey the sleeping conditions with bunks in tiers. I found myself longing for the 'ovens' and the 'chambers' – surely here I would have a taste of the authentic. The ovens were impeccable – well–blacked iron in bricks with a wreath laid by a British regiment in 1977.

'You know when they opened the doors, all the bodies fell out. They had been climbing on top of each other in a desperate attempt to get air.'

‘Just the sort of thing I didn’t want to know’ said my young student companion.

There were other relics but of the countless millions of Jews there was almost no sign. It was as though they had never passed through these gentle poplar lined avenues.

Several summers, I had French students to stay for a two week immersion experience. I provided accommodation,(ie son moved out of his room) taught them in the morning and arranged things for them to do and see in the afternoon. We were always sad to see them go even though I was in a near- state of collapse after all the cooking and outings and entertainment.

And so son and I negotiated the processes of teenage growing up. I remember thinking when he was 13 that this was no problem at all. But soon after I changed my mind. I think the worst problem was the teenage drinking which I knew I could control only if the other mums felt the same. They, however, had a more laissez faire attitude and there was little I could do on my own. Totnes on Friday and Saturday nights was awash with teenagers wandering the streets. Gangs from Torquay came in and there were fights between the Hippies and the Kevs. The underagers hung about the civic square until they were old enough to congregate in the many bars. As my flat was central it made a very convenient stopover. Somehow we got through without too much trauma.

And gradually son left the nest with a Newquay trip with friends here and a winter job in the Alps there. For several years we ended up in the flat at the same time, some of the time, but by 1995, when he was 20, I was free for the first time in many years, maybe ever, to be completely on my own in France. I have written of this experience of the first year in France elsewhere.* it ended with meeting Keith who happily agreed to join me in further adventure.

I have made little mention of my daughter. After university, she too made for the Alps and some time later when she had returned to Edinburgh she met a man who soon afterwards left for Canada. She went out to join him and 10 years later they took Canadian citizenship and now have two Canadian children.

*Second Spring 2013 available on Lulu or as an ebook on Smashwords.

13

Pakistan interlude 2007-8

Keith was as enchanted as I was by the day to day French village life. There were a few months of tooing and froing on his part. We toured round looking at houses we might buy and imagined what life would be like together in a nearly new house perched on a bit of a ridge with views, or in a Gascon L shaped farmhouse with bags of character and lots of land, or a smaller house with some character and not much land that would need minimal looking after. Keith made an offer but in the 7 day cooling off period got panicky and withdrew it. Really I was attached to my village house and to the village itself. It was and is a mediaeval bastide town with a village square surrounded by thick oak timber colonnades. But the right house was not to be found.

During the winter of 2006 I stayed with my cat Maimai waiting for the right rabies resistant level to be reached. He didn't go out much and continued to be a lesson in how to grow old gracefully. When we finally went back in June I was able to sit with him in the back whilst Keith drove. Even so Maimai suffered.

Meanwhile, a new adventure beckoned. Keith had always wanted to respond to a work colleague's appeal to go and help out in Pakistan. I had for a long time thought that at the end of my career I would return to a sort of VSO experience in Africa. This seemed like the opportunity I had been looking for. There had been a connection between Gloucester University and a small Kashmir educational charity for some time.

KEF (Kashmir Education Foundation) was founded by a Kashmiri family of four brothers all in their 80's and 90's. As village lads initially they went to school under a tree, but they had been noticed during the British raj and been given a pukka British education at a residential school two days walk away.

They had been trained to become leaders. One became the head of a bank, another was the head of Forestry in Kashmir and two had gone into the army where one became one of five top generals. They had met up at the time of their mother's funeral and decided to put something back into the community. They sacrificed their orchard with rare apple trees to provide land for a primary school. It was to be equally available to girls as well as boys and to be a school of high quality again with the aim of bringing up children who would bring on the level of the country. It was so successful that the children demanded to continue at the end of primary education and so a secondary school was built and then came the question of training teachers so a teacher training facility was set up.

For ease of access to prospective visiting donors the teacher training institute had been set up in a Punjabi village on the plains within easy reach of Islamabad airport. It had depended very much on VSO staffing but since the last Director left there was something of a gap and the idea was that Keith would be the Director for a period of time to get things on a more formal footing. I was simply an add-on and it was agreed I would be useful teaching English.

In April we went out to Pakistan for two weeks for an introductory visit. We were met by the Brigadier (retired), a charming, simple man who pointed out the significance of lacklustre concrete buildings we passed before being swept into a good quality hotel which had only a little reference to its locale. The heat told us we were in the tropics. A non-stop induction programme had been arranged with a certain military efficiency. We went to the

Institute where we were to be based several times, we visited a teacher training college in Lahore where it was so hot we had to duck out of a sightseeing trip to the border ceremony where Indian and Pakistani soldiers parade in opposition, but we did see the Moghul gardens and the red fort.

Our trip to see the original school complex up in Kashmir was one of the highlights. Once we had left Islamabad behind we passed by Muree which is higher and cooler and had something of a colonial past. We were driven past forests and busy villages with open shops selling foodstuffs or hardware household necessities or meat. There was lots of corrugated iron. Leaving a village behind the trail might go down to a river and then snake up again and so on up and down. On entering Kashmir itself we showed our passes which the Brig had obtained for us. The road in parts had been affected by mudslides. There was very little traffic and that was mostly lorries splendidly painted with intricate panels. All the time we were gaining height until six hours later we reached a land of terraces, mountains, and pine trees some 6,000 feet up.

Kashmir was divided between India and Pakistan at the time of independence in 1947. It is a bitter bone of contention between the two countries. Pakistan

Kashmir (Azad or free Kashmir as it is called) has a lot of independence from Pakistan and Kashmiris often refer to Pakistan as a different country. The Kashmiris are known for their robustness and independence and respectful attitude to women so that it was no coincidence that the brothers thought educating women was the way forward. At times the Kashmiris have fought to reunite the Indian and Pakistani areas and at the last war a line of control some ten miles away from the school was drawn up. The brothers' dream is to set up schools of high quality all over Pakistan and to create an educated work force that will lift Pakistan out of poverty whilst retaining the very moral standard that comes from their religious background.

We arrived at a very impressive building (it was so well built that it was the only one in the immediate area to survive the 2005 earthquake). We were accommodated in a hostel attached to the school and stayed a few days. We took walks on the village paths through the trees and could only respond to some of the many invitations to take tea. The brothers' family house was almost restored after the earthquake of three years before. Even without that information, it would have been impossible to ignore the earthquake. People were keen to tell us how they had survived, and everywhere there were traces of cracks in buildings like the local hospital, or the corrugated shelters which had enabled people to survive the severe Kashmiri winter. When it was clear that the school itself had endured, it was made into a rescue centre and the younger members of the brothers' families had arranged for the shelters to be constructed and distributed but they had to be dug into a four foot pit. People were wandering around dazed and unable to focus on this task and it came to a point where the distributors had to threaten to leave. This was a turning point it seemed and people were galvanised into action and so got their new shelters. The family were at pains to point out how this sort of community aid had been so much more useful than the international community swanning round in huge vehicles making assessments. Indeed the charity has subsequently been very conscientious in responding to disasters in other parts of the country using their extensive network of contacts.

Back in Rawalpindi we stayed with the General (retired), one of the brothers who had founded the charity and met some of his impressive and extensive family. It was expected that we would live in rented accommodation in Islamabad where we could join 'The Club' and commute out to the Institute (some one hour's drive away) each day. We said we would be happy to come out if they still wanted us but were sorry that we were not prepared to commute. Okay, they said, we will build you a house on the campus.

But what about Maimai? I read an encouraging book by a journalist who had had many overseas posts and wrote a book called 'The Cat that travelled the World'. Maimai was now 19 and even the thought of him travelling between England and France was a major trauma so the idea of taking him with us was never a starter. An appeal to my network of friends yielded no-one who would be prepared to take him on. We made an abortive journey to Edinburgh where Keith's aged stepmother liked the idea of having him but faced with the reality backed out. There seemed nothing for it but to enjoy our last month together and then have the vet come and put him down. An appointment was duly made for a Friday a week before we were due to fly out. On the Wednesday, a friend from Brittany rang up as she mistakenly thought I had rung her. When I explained this and that and that we were going to have to say goodbye to Mai, she immediately offered to have him. A few phone calls later and we had a crossing to Roscoff and Mai made his last journey. I was so relieved to leave him in loving hands.

We asked if we could begin our stay in Kashmir as in September it was still uncomfortably hot down on the Plains and the acting principal at the teacher training institute was not due to go until the December. In this way we eased ourselves into the situation. We gave workshops to the staff and did some teacher observations and I had small English conversation sessions with the teachers most of whom had been trained by VSO teachers on the plains. After some six weeks we were ready for action and descended from the mountains to stay in Rawalpindi with the General – one of the four brothers. Despite having had two heart bypass operations, he tirelessly worked for his Charity whose head office was within walking distance. Every morning we got up around 6.00am, had a lift to a pickup point where the school minibus took us and several other staff out to the Institute. It was a rather nerve wracking journey along busy roads with traffic making for loopholes in what seemed a chaotic and frantic dash. Classes began in a slightly haphazard way. Really our task was to get things a bit more orderly. There were some 40 students just finishing their one year training with teaching practice in several different schools back in Pindi.

They were teaching in an English medium which was quite difficult for them as most of them had only learnt by rote and passed exams by repeating what they had read. The level of English speaking was something they were keen to improve and we were hugely welcomed as a resource for this.

During that autumn term we were certainly learning as much about the students and the system as they were learning about, or with, us. Our main task was to set up the mechanism for selecting the next batch of students who were due to start at the beginning of the next year. The local staff together with the new VSO took on the selection procedure and my main contribution was to design an intensive language course for the first 6 weeks. And so frameworks began to be established. The curriculum for each subject was codified, and the course eventually assessed and recognised by the University in Islamabad.

Come December, we were weary of the daily journeys too and from the campus and we started to make noises about the time it was taking for the house built on the campus to be completed. Much to the envy of our Pakistani pupils and friends we took off for India for the Christmas break. Like so many parts of the world where there are arbitrary territorial divisions, the Pakistani people I met would have loved to interact with their Indian neighbours and vice versa. I obtained a pass to enter the heavily guarded diplomatic zone in Islamabad to obtain visas. Formalities completed, there was a comfortable ride to Lahore by train, followed by a rickshaw to the border. The computer had to be switched on to record our journey in the brand new building and coffee was served whilst we waited in the empty hall. Then we walked the 70 yards or to a ramshackle hut on the Indian side and got our bearings amidst the lorries crammed with tomatoes, vegetables and Sikh drivers waiting to get into Pakistan. On to the tumult of Amritsar, a night in a hotel, the Golden Temple, women on motorbikes and the buzz of an Indian city so unlike the restraint of Lahore and Pindi.

Keith had done VSO in North India in his early twenties and we deviated slightly from the train journey to Delhi to revisit his school and village. Much had of course changed in the 45 years that had gone by. Ironically the school was part of the military and the boys he taught would have become the very generals that 'our' general and military had fought against. We then revisited a place that had been so important to me - the Osho meditation ashram in Poona.

It had been 12 years since I visited the ashram and it too had gone through many changes. We stayed a good week, much of which I wasted making comparisons with what had been. Osho had died in 1990 some 18 years previously and the place was run by a committee – a structure he had himself set up in his last year. The large marble floor with a tented roof where Osho had arrived most mornings and evenings by Rolls Royce from his house 50 yards away was just an open space, a shadow of its former self and used for events or Bollywood dancing. The individual and group sessions were now priced at European, indeed German rates so that a massage cost more than it would have done back home. What I had appreciated in former days as the accessibility of therapy was now only an elitist opportunity. Still Keith got to see the place and thoroughly enjoyed reading and sitting beside the pool. Prompted by Keith we also did a tourist trip out of Poona and spent a night at Ajanta and saw the temples built into rock. For me the spirit of the place – ie Osho – had gone and left a vacuum. Yet others who remained part of the community and who had visited more frequently felt the vibe had continued. We spent a couple of nights on trains returning to Amritsar, Lahore, and by airconditioned bus back to Pindi where after a few more nights with the general we were able to move into our new accommodation.

Installed in our new house – we had the ground floor and the VSO had the upper floor, we combined domesticity with our work. Life became routinised. Classes began soon after 8.00am. We were rather over-staffed as with the new academic year student numbers had dropped to half. This was a direct result of lack of finance. Earlier cohorts were subsidised heavily by KEF but this year the subsidy was not possible. I reduced my teaching commitment after the six week intensive so that other staff had something to do! I did however, arrange afternoon out of school activities mainly rounders. The weeks passed by culminating with the diploma ceremony when the girls decorated the hall with wonderful large art works, plays and songs were performed, visitors came, a tent – shamayana was put up – and food of all sorts served. This time for security, guards were installed on the flat rooves.

We had planned initially to stay for two years but things were just beginning to heat up. Every Friday suicide bombers sent themselves and some other unfortunates to paradise. At first these were attacks on the military especially in Rawalpindi which is a military garrison town, but when an aid agency got attacked we and the Charity got nervous. I wanted to return. We felt in some ways that we had done our job and were really pleased when a new Director, was found. We left expecting to return from time to time. Unfortunately the Taliban situation only got worse and the time we allocated for a month's visit the following year had to be postponed indefinitely. This was not just for our safety but also for the safety of the project where Europeans would have attracted unwelcome attention. We maintain contact, however, and occasionally organise fund raising activities to subsidise would- be students at the Institute.

14

France for ever?

In November 2008 Keith bought his French house. It stood out in the centre of a village with a ground and two upper floors. Its white walls with ox blood shutters were more the colours of the Bearn, a region to the West, than the Haute Pyrenees. It sported two balconies and was described by one of our visitors as being like a house in Surrey. With its five bedrooms it would, however, have cost something like five times the price. It had been built in the 1930's by a banker and had been largely unoccupied for a number of years. It had a not–too-big garden with some ancient trees and an L shaped plot where we could start a vegetable garden.

It was the twenty sixth house we looked at (including the houses we had seen the previous year most of which were no longer available.) We had been sightseeing in a wine growing area further north when I happened to see a house for sale with an agent's board. Idly surfing the agent's internet site that evening for further details led to a dead end as far as that house was concerned but I saw another house in 'our' area which seemed very reasonable considering the kitchen and bathroom had been done up and there was what looked like another small house in its grounds. A visit was organised to a village half an hour's drive away from my village house and half an hour nearer the mountains. Keith was not impressed. Certainly it was not the L shaped Gascon farmhouse we and most other expats aspired to. And the village was some 5 km away from a shop (Intermarché) and a further 2 km on from a larger village where on et day we had already established meeting up with a number of ex-pats – Brits mainly but a sprinkling of Dutch, German and others. I appreciated the possibilities at first sight. The house faced south and every time we visited the sun was out hence we called it 'The Sunny House' as opposed to other contenders, 'The Dream House', 'The Authentic house' and 'The Blue house'. The house was in a long valley stretching north/ south to the Pyrenees and bounded by ridges on either side. It looked out on one side to a gentle green hill with woods. A little down the road ***was*** a handsome Gascon farmhouse, home to a herd of cream coloured cows when they were not grazing in the fields. A few yards on was the farmhouse itself opposite the church. If you walked in the other direction, and looked beyond the maize fields and clumps of trees surrounding separate houses that formed part of the spread out village you could, most days, see the Pic du Midi amidst the Pyrenean panorama.

Keith had a choice between paying off his mortgage in UK or retaining it and using the money instead to buy a house outright. Buying a house round here is like most things slow, however, in this case, we had to jump as there was another buyer in the offing who was applying for a mortgage. As a cash buyer Keith was at an advantage. Things happened quickly as we had already booked to return to the UK in a few week's time. The widow from whom we bought the house was almost in tears as she looked around what would have been her and her husband's retirement project. He had died several years before whilst helping a friend back a tractor. He ended up underneath.

These kind of accidental deaths are not so uncommon out here. A friend's husband has three relatives who have died as a result of rural tragedies; one was also killed by a tractor, one was struck by lightning, and one was shot while hunting. When I called on her lately it was to find that her sister-in law's mother had been gored by a cow and was in hospital. There was a couple with whom we played Belote (a card game). The man loved to hunt and fish. One weekend he had gone hunting alone and did not return. He was found dead having shot himself. It seems he tripped whilst his gun was loaded. Though no-one quite knows.

And so began a quite idyllic existence.

First of all came the cats - Matisse and Jyoti – brother and sister. Their mother lived across the road, a home she shared with a number of other pedigree looking creatures with silky thick cream fur. In the afternoons she mingled with a farmyard of creatures that were let out when their owner who lived some 13 miles away with another tribe of cats, came to look after them. They lived in the barns and outhouses surrounding the owner's unoccupied ancestral home. The owner's mother had been born there. It was her grandmother's house and although she seemed to have little intention of ever moving back, she was modernising the place little by little with a respect for all things ancient and familial. We shared a common interest in the past and loved to hear her tales of how things used to be in this once thriving village.

The father of the cats came from our nearer neighbours whose garden adjoined ours. He was a rather scraggy black and white farm cat. Matisse and Jyoti were hence a cross between the two with farm cat ings. Jyoti's ings had slipped slightly across her face giving her a slightly fashionable air whilst Matisse, was a magnificent grey and white with deep fur and a deep purr. We had them very young as the mother kept hiding them in the grass for protection and the owner was afraid they would be eaten before she could find them.

A year later came the chickens. I wanted chickens that I could enjoy looking at and at first could see only rather dull ones with feathers missing round their necks. But then a Dutch woman said she had masses of chickens and would be delighted if we took some away and yes they were beautiful. So we acquired a young cock, who had not yet started to crow, a mother with her day old chick, Belle who was very beautiful but rather cantankerous and Fleur who was almost white and gave us many eggs before she got sick and one night died. The following spring Tiny (the one day old) was not to be seen. We searched everywhere. After 8 days she turned up none the worse for wear, ate heartily, had a deep dust bath and then disappeared. Finally it clicked; she had gone broody but where? We kept a minute watch on her another day and in the blink of an eye she was gone again. Finally she emerged out of a tree stump followed by her two chicks. So sweet! Then Belle sat on a big clutch of eggs under the roof of the chicken house which was insulated with straw. 21 days later at midday – all very textbook – there were some 13 chicks falling all over the place. We helped her to get them down to the ground and a stall of her own. What to do with them all? We found ourselves in the same position as the woman who gave us her chickens- delighted when someone took seven of them off us. Tiny then produced two more – both cocks – and the fate of them hung in the balance. We had already managed to find two cocks a home whilst sadly three went into the neighbour's pot. Really they were an endless source of amusement and amazement. There was quite a period when most of them refused to go in at night and perched instead in the walnut tree forcing Keith when the weather turned nasty to prize them off in the dark. Then they each organised their own egg laying place, only one laid her egg in the 'proper' place as in the nesting box we had made. Vinney, our magnificent cock would donate grapes we gave him to his harem of hens and stand guard over them while they ate. Keith particularly liked their company while he was digging when they would snatch worms in a most daring way.

Then there were people. We were both keen on 'integrating'. Thus our French course continued to be as important as ever and we made erratic progress with plenty of plateaus on the way. We joined a badminton club, danced once a week in the winter with a French folkdance group in a nearby village, Keith joined a French choir, and we joined a rambling group in another nearby village. These experiences all had their moments. I don't think we met a single unfriendly person. The weekly Belote was, as explained, curtailed very tragically.

Gradually we came to know the villagers. The maire was very busy with his enterprise. What appeared outwardly to be a rather smartly done up Gascon L shaped farmhouse was on closer inspection, a highly specialised precision metalwork business employing 12 men in uniform overalls. Alongside was the house with a flourishing garden, geothermal heating in a field and a smart wife who was to be seen bottling huge amounts of green beans in the summer. In his leisure time he told us, amongst other pursuits, he took off for canyoning in Spain. It was impossible he admitted for him to speak slowly. Once a week for an hour or so he was available in the mairie almost next door to us where he acted on messages filtered by his secretary. He was very jovial and aside from occasional meetings in the road, we saw him only at village events, for aperos around New Year time when he responded to our invitation and occasionally about formalities. We understood about a quarter of his jokes eg ‘Oh so you do the formalities for marriages?’ (us, context of a village wedding’,

Well its better than doing the formalities for a death!’(which he did also).

Our immediate neighbours (them of the cat’s father) were treasures. Now in their 70’s they had close connections with the village though they had spent their working lives in the Creuze area. Sylvie was born in what had been the next-door house, now relegated to a barn after her parents in the 60-s built a modern bungalow nearby. They both had led active lives as farmers and running a hotel and they continued to manage several vegetable plots such that they were self-sufficient in vegetables. They were very involved with their children’s families although the grandchildren lived a long way away.

To some extent we initiated meetings which were then reciprocated and one thing led to another so that little by little we came to know about a quarter of the other 113 residents. Some had been touched by the German occupation. Two children had been adopted: - there was a very black boy from Bukeima Fasso and a teenage girl (adopted at four months from Chile) who came to interview us for the census. Simply by needing things to be done we encountered other villagers. We needed some roof tiles, we needed a new septic tank, a tree to be cut down and planked and so on. We met others by attending the annual village events in particular the chasse meal which took place over 6 hours. Our neighbours included us in family celebrations around their Golden Wedding. I myself organised a fundraising event for KEF to which a number of people in the village came as well as the wider, mainly expat, community.

As well as the people we sought out the history and there were several people who were happy to describe how the village used to be. In its heyday it had two cafés, a ropemaker, a forge, a shoemaker, and until 1928 an agricultural college. In earlier times there had been a castle. This had burned down and been replaced by a second which had been demolished to avoid a window tax in the 1920's. A local historian had pieced some of this history together and put it on the internet. We were anxious to track down photos of the big oak tree which had stood on the corner of what was now our house and round which people had danced on July 14th.

As well as being open to newcomers – we were joined by another English couple and other families who were new to the village before – there were those families who had lived there for generations and whose family name had given rise to the name of the road. All the old families had been farmers. There were also several houses that had passed down to younger generations who no longer lived there. The houses were well looked after but empty. This sense of a respect for roots extended into the graveyard where (as in most of France probably), the graves are decorated on Toussaint–All Saints Day– in November. Hence whenever there is a burial and most of the villagers are involved, all are reminded of their ancestors who are lying there. We found ourselves in one half year attending two funerals, and two masses.

The seasons were ers and led to different rhythms and pursuits. The winters were short but could be severe for two or three weeks. It was a time to stay by the fire as much as possible and try to maintain some sort of heat for the animals. It was also a time to have trips out to the mountains on sunny days when the snow up there was thick but sufficiently sparse at home that the roads were usable. By spring the garden needed attention and this lasted until the autumn. We had huge pumpkins, huge parsnips, a hedge of peas, lots of beans courgettes etc. thanks to very fertile soil which had not been cultivated for many years. We planted an apple tree and a peach tree and picked and bottled cherries from two old trees.

We had raspberries, strawberries and grapes ourselves but were given quinces, figs and mirabelles which all had to be eaten or bottled or made into jam so what with all that and visitors and holidays, village fetes and vide greniers (car boot sales) the summer was a busy time.

There was a five year plan to stay with a view to returning to be near grandchildren (Keith's) and to pass our dotage free from language constraints. But after about three years we were aware of a question hanging over us? Where were we going to be ending our days? Were we going back to a country which seemed so crowded and tiresomely inefficient? Would we try out a more on/off time with six months here and six months there? What about our cats? Not to mention all the financial ins and outs of straddling two residences and two countries. We never doubted the quality of life in the village and for both of us the sense of plenty, and the spirit of generosity this engendered among those we met, were something we found missing on our return to the mother country where people were chasing their tails so hard that they had little time for connecting or reflecting. Perhaps too they were envious that we had somehow managed to escape? It seemed that what many of our friends strived for existed here in abundance.

As a resident I found out that I could reserve my patch in the churchyard for a nominal fee. Although the path to the churchyard was not clear, it was good to know that that was where it could end.

Made in the USA
Charleston, SC
10 April 2014